D0952112

DIEGO RIVERA

His Art, His Life

DIEGO RIVERA

His Art, His Life

Doreen Gonzales

Enslow Publishers, Inc.

40 Industrial Road	PO Box 38
Box 398	Aldershot
Berkeley Heights, NJ 07922	Hants GU12 6BP
USA	UK

http://www.enslow.com

Library of Congress Cataloging-in-Publication Data

Gonzales, Doreen.
    Diego Rivera : his art, his life / Doreen Gonzales.
       p. cm. — (Hispanic biographies)
    Includes bibliographical references and index.
    Summary: A biography of the noted Mexican muralist discussing his art, his
political ties, and his relationship with the painter Frida Kahlo.
    ISBN 0-89490-764-6
    1. Rivera, Diego, 1886–1957—Juvenile literature. 2. Painters—
Mexico—Biography—Juvenile literature. [1. Rivera, Diego, 1886-1957. 2. Artists.]
I. Title. II. Series.
ND259.R5G67 1996
759.972—dc20
    [B]   96-861
                                           CIP
                                         AC

Printed in the United States of America

10 9 8 7 6 5 4 3

Illustration Credits: Archivo Cenidiap-INBA, Mexico City, Mexico, pp. 20,
33; Instituto Nacional de Bellas Artes, Mexico City, Mexico, pp. 46, 99, 103;
Library of Congress, Prints and Photographs Division, Carl Van Vechten
Collection, p. 73; Leo Tanguma, pp. 110, 111; Library of Congress, Prints and
Photographs Division, Carl Van Vechten Collection and Instituto Nacional de
Bellas Artes, Mexico City, Mexico, pp. 12, 13, 85; Peter A. Juley and Son
Collection, National Museum of American Art, Smithsonian Institution, pp.
59, 66, 93; Photograph © The Detroit Institute of Arts, 1995, Gift of Edsel B.
Ford and Instituto Nacional de Bellas Artes, Mexico City, Mexico, pp. 77, 79.

Cover Illustration: Peter A. Juley and Son Collection, National Museum of
American Art, Smithsonian Institution

CONTENTS

RIVERA, THE MURALIST

 Each stroke of Diego Rivera's paintbrush brought him closer to a dream. The idea for this picture had been planted in Rivera's childhood, and it had grown with him throughout his life. Now, in 1929, the forty-three-year-old artist's vision was beginning to blossom. Rivera was painting murals at his nation's capitol, the National Palace, in Mexico City, Mexico. In six enormous paintings, Rivera illustrated important events in Mexico's history from 1500 to the 1900s. His grand work was entitled "The History of Mexico: From the Conquest to the Future."

Rivera's murals were not just portraits of famous people, though. The artist wanted his National Palace murals to be a tribute to Mexico's ordinary citizens.[1] Many of these Mexicans were descended from people who had lived in Mexico since ancient times.

Like the Native Americans in the United States, people native to Mexico came to be called Indians. Indians can also be referred to as indigenous people. The word indigenous means someone or something that is native to a certain land region. Several different groups of indigenous people lived in Mexico before Europeans arrived there in the 1500s. Among them were the Olmecs, Mayans, and Toltecs. In his National Palace murals, Rivera also highlighted another one of Mexico's indigenous populations, the Aztecs. The Aztec culture flourished during the 1300s and 1400s. It was rich and complex. It was also warlike, and the Aztecs conquered many other native groups. Their territory extended across south-central Mexico with a great capitol city in the center called Tenochtitlán.

In 1519, a Spanish explorer named Hernando Cortés led the first Europeans into Mexico. These Spanish soldiers, known as conquistadors, marched from Mexico's eastern gulf coast to Tenochtitlán. There they encountered the Aztec emperor, Montezuma, who tried to appease the Spaniards with gifts of gold. But Cortés wanted more. He claimed the land and its people as the property of Spain. War followed.

The Aztecs were a powerful nation among other indigenous Mexicans, but they were not as strong as the
Spaniards. This was mostly because the Spaniards
possessed two weapons the Aztecs had never seen before—guns and horses. These gave the conquistadors
a huge advantage, and by 1521, the Aztec empire had
been conquered. Spain became the ruler of the land,
and Cortés built his headquarters over the destroyed
city of Tenochtitlán. Several years later, Mexico's capitol, the National Palace, would be built on the same site.

For the next three centuries, Spain governed
Mexico. During this time, the Spaniards enslaved the
natives and forced them to convert to the religion of
Spain, Roman Catholicism. The Spaniards brought
Africans to Mexico and enslaved them, too. The
Spanish government then enacted laws that
discriminated against people of African and native
Mexican descent. Social status became based on a
person's ancestral background. People of pure
Spanish ancestry were considered better than other
citizens. The lowest class of citizen was the African,
closely followed by the indigenous people. As time
passed, though, there were marriages between some
Spaniards, indigenous Mexicans, and Africans. These
couples had children of blended ancestry who were
called *mestizos*, meaning people of mixed heritage.
After the Spanish entered Mexico, mestizos became a
constantly growing segment of the population.

By the early 1800s, many mestizos had grown tired of foreign rule. They, along with certain other groups in Mexican society, longed for independence from Spain. In 1810, a priest named Miguel Hidalgo began a revolt against Spain in the little town of Dolores, Mexico. Although it suffered many setbacks, the rebellion eventually spread and gained momentum. In 1821, Spain finally surrendered, and the independent country of Mexico was born. Unfortunately, the Mexican people were still not truly free. Now a series of dictators ruled the land, causing Mexicans to revolt again in 1910.

Diego Rivera's murals at the National Palace showed several of these events from Mexico's history. He painted Aztecs tending their fields of corn and worshipping one of their most revered gods, Quetzalcóatl. Rivera showed conquistadors on their horses, battling Aztecs. He painted the leaders of Mexico's first war for independence, including Father Hidalgo holding chains that symbolized Mexico's bondage to Spain. Then Rivera painted the revolutionary leaders of the early 1900s.

Rivera's mural covers more than twenty-six hundred square feet of wall space over an enormous staircase in the National Palace. Every inch of this area is filled with life-size portraits of people in action. One historic episode after another is pictured, each one butting against the next in a collage that sometimes crosses centuries. Even so, the mural does not seem confusing. Rivera's expert use of color and composition guides the viewer's eyes from one scene to the next. The artistic qualities of the murals, though, are only a part of their tremendous worth. Rivera's National Palace paintings are also important because they proclaim pride in Mexico's native heritage, and they do so in Mexico's most important public building.

When Mexico won its independence from Spain, many of the legal discriminatory practices against native Africans and Mexicans and mestizos ended. But people continued to look down on these groups and discriminate against them. During the early 1900s, some citizens began challenging these prejudices. Many artists criticized discrimination, and Diego Rivera was one of the time's most vocal artists. In a country that had long slighted its native heritage, Rivera's National Palace murals glorified the country's indigenous populations. For instance, Rivera placed an eagle at the center of his staircase murals. The eagle carried an Aztec banner in its beak, a banner that represented war, defiance, and pride. Eagles were honored omens in Aztec mythology. According to legend, it was an eagle that guided the Aztecs to the site of Tenochtitlán. This symbol, along with other symbols in the murals, was a clear and powerful tribute to Mexico's native population.

These two pages show a portion of Rivera's mural "The History of Mexico," which was painted above the staircase at the National Palace in Mexico City. Along the bottom, mounted conquistadors fight Aztec warriors.

Far to the right, guns and a cannon belch flames. Scenes of religious conversions and the destruction of the indigenous Mexican culture fill the center space. At the top, Rivera painted portraits of famous people from Mexican history.

Furthermore, Rivera's murals honored the everyday people who formed the foundation of Mexican society. Interspersed among generals and famous leaders from Mexico's history were warriors, slaves, farmers, and soldiers. These people, Rivera seemed to be saying, were also an indispensable part of the nation's development. The location of Rivera's tribute to ordinary Mexicans was especially significant. Because the murals were painted in a public building, anyone could view them, regardless of their ancestry or financial status. In addition, the thousands of Mexican citizens who could not read could look at the pictures and see the vital role their ancestors had played in forming their country. Rivera's murals have even been called "a history textbook in pictures."[2] Today, the National Palace murals are still one of the largest and most complete visual accounts of any nation's history.[3]

Actually, Rivera created many outstanding paintings during his life. Since childhood, art had been his one true passion, and he had sacrificed much to pursue it. He had lived in poverty in order to become an artist and had often put art before his family and his friends. In fact, nearly every waking hour of Rivera's life had revolved around art. For many years, he worked fourteen hours a day, and when he was not painting, he was sketching on scraps of paper he had tucked into his pocket for just such an occasion. By the time Rivera began work at the National Palace, he had already invested nearly thirty years in the scholarly study and daily practice of art. Rivera, however, had no regrets. During the later years of his life, he once commented, "the most joyous moments of my life were those I had spent in painting."[4] In turn, Rivera's art brought joy to others. Today his work is still admired by people all over the world, and Diego Rivera is remembered as one of the best artists of the twentieth century.[5]

THE YOUNG
ARTIST

On December 8, 1886, twin boys were born in Guanajuato, Mexico, to Diego and María Rivera. One of them would grow up to be a world famous artist. Soon after his birth, this baby was christened with the many names of his ancestors. Perhaps it was a sign of things to come that he should be given such a grandiose name: Diego María de la Concepción Juan Nepomuceno Estanislao de la Rivera y Barrientos Acosta y Rodríguez.

Baby Diego's parents were well educated and financially secure. They lived in the heart of Guanajuato, a mining town located in the hills of central Mexico. Diego Rivera, a large, bearded man, was of Spanish, Portuguese, and Jewish ancestry. María Rivera was a small woman of Spanish and native Mexican heritage. In 1888, Diego's twin brother became ill and died. To distract herself from grief over his death, Diego's mother entered medical school to become an obstetrician.[1] An obstetrician is a doctor who specializes in pregnancy and childbirth.

In the meantime, Diego's father worked as an inspector of rural schools. As part of his job, he made frequent trips to schools in remote areas of the countryside. On these journeys, Rivera saw people living in terrible poverty. Their misery saddened him, and he decided to help them.[2] So he began describing the needy in a weekly newspaper he published. His articles regularly asked rich people to help the poor.

Rivera's appeals for the needy were generally ignored. Mexico's president, Porfirio Díaz, had made laws that kept rich people wealthy and poor people poor. For example, Díaz allowed a small number of men to take land from indigenous communities and poor farmers. By combining several small plots, these men created large ranches for themselves. These huge ranches were called *haciendas*. Hacienda owners often employed the very poor whose land they had taken and then paid them terrible wages. Consequently, the workers could not always afford food and housing, and often had to borrow money from the hacienda owners simply to survive. Then the owners would not allow the workers to leave the hacienda until their debts were paid. In this way, the workers became virtual slaves, and the owners kept a steady supply of cheap labor. President Díaz also permitted mine and factory owners to pay their employees extremely low wages while expecting them to work in horrible conditions. When these workers organized any kind of a protest against their bad treatment, President Díaz sent soldiers from the Mexican army to quiet them.

Most of Mexico's wealthy citizens supported President Díaz because his policies kept them rich. The poor supported him, too, partly because anyone who spoke out against the president was punished. Many people, therefore, preferred to tolerate the government and avoid people with ideas like Diego's father. Yet Rivera continued to call on the wealthy to help the poor. He even criticized the Roman Catholic Church for not doing enough for the poverty-stricken. This was another unpopular stance. Most Mexicans were devout Catholics, and their fear of God kept them from challenging the church.

To complicate the matter, the Catholic Church had once ruled Mexico. Although the Church's governing authority had been greatly reduced by the time Diego was born, it was still a powerful political force. The close connection between the Church and the government made many Mexicans feel that opposition to the government was almost the same thing as opposition to the Church—and opposition to the Church was like opposition to God. This made criticism of the government nearly as unthinkable as criticism of God. Many people viewed Rivera's political beliefs as blasphemy. Among those were María Rivera's aunt and sister. They, too, lived in the Rivera's Guanajuato home. To keep peace in the household, the adults had worked out an agreement regarding their differing beliefs. Rivera allowed the women to practice Catholicism without his interference. In return, they were not to teach Diego anything about religion. Consequently, the boy was not taken to church, but received his moral education from his father.

All of Diego's early education, in fact, came from his father. When he was four, Rivera taught him to read, using books that were around the house. Diego later said he particularly enjoyed his mother's medical textbooks because they helped him understand how the body worked. Actually, learning how anything worked was one of Diego's first loves. He was fascinated by machinery, including the mining equipment that dotted Guanajuato's hillsides and the trains that rumbled through its railroad station. This love of mechanical objects earned the young boy the nickname, "the engineer."[3]

Diego Rivera at about four years of age. It appears that he is clutching a toy train in his left hand.

Little Diego had another interest. He liked to draw. Initially, he marked on the walls and furniture of the house. To prevent this, his father covered one room in canvas, making Diego an art studio where he could draw wherever and whenever he pleased. Not surprisingly, his favorite things to draw were machines, mines, and trains. One of Diego's oldest surviving drawings is of a locomotive chugging uphill followed by its caboose.

When Diego was five years old, his mother gave birth to a girl, María. The next year, Diego's mother was ready to take her final tests to become an obstetrician. Before the examinations, one aunt secretly took Diego to church to pray for her success. Unfamiliar with the custom of praying to symbols, Diego could not understand why the worshippers seemed to think there was power in the statues that were scattered around the sanctuary. He decided that the people in the church must be ignorant. "Suddenly," he later remembered, "rage possessed me, and I ran from my aunt and climbed up the steps of the altar. Then at the top of my voice, I began to address the astonished worshippers."[4] Diego told the people that they were stupid and crazy. Several started screaming, thinking that Diego must be possessed by evil. Even the priest tried to quiet Diego, who had frightened everyone in the church. Finally, Diego's aunt got him out the door.[5]

In spite of Diego's outburst at the church, his mother passed her tests and became one of Guanajuato's first female obstetricians. Diego's scene did affect the family, though. The family was already unpopular in the town because of Rivera's liberal beliefs about the government. After Diego's incident at the church, people liked the family less. When Diego was almost seven years old, the Riveras moved to Mexico City.

In the capitol city, Diego was struck by scarlet fever, then typhoid, and he was too ill to draw for nearly a year. Once he recovered, he was sent to his first school. It was a Catholic school that his mother insisted he attend. Predictably, Diego did not fit in. He soon transferred to a different school, and although it was also a Catholic school, it seemed to suit Diego better.

Meanwhile, Diego became interested in art again. He created a miniature army by pasting drawings of soldiers onto cardboard. Diego played constantly with these "troops," acting out military battle plans he had already worked through on paper.[6] Diego also developed an interest in his aunt's collection of silver jewelry and ceramic sculptures. Because most of them were religious, the aunt saw his curiosity as an opportunity to take him to church, where there was more artwork. Diego went with her to see the art, but unlike their visit to the Guanajuato sanctuary, this outing passed peacefully and pleasantly.

By the time Diego was ten years old, he knew he wanted to be an artist.[7] While other children played with toys or out-of-doors, Diego drew and painted. He convinced his mother to enroll him in evening art classes at the famous Mexico City art school, the San Carlos Academy of Fine Arts. During the day, Diego attended his regular school. He was a bright student, and his teachers passed him through the grades more quickly than the other children. At night he studied art. In 1899, Diego began school at San Carlos Academy full time. Only twelve years old, he was one of the youngest students there. One classmate later remembered how Diego sometimes arrived at school with his pockets bursting with treasures he had collected along the way. Occasionally, this included an earthworm or two.[8]

San Carlos Academy was a traditional art school that used European teaching techniques. This meant students spent a lot of time copying famous artwork to learn how to paint and draw. In addition, they took classes in perspective, geometry, and architecture to make their work look realistic. Diego also took a course in anatomy, the study of the human body. Understanding the structure of the body would help him draw people that looked real. Although he was still very young, Diego showed enough talent to be taught by some of Mexico's greatest artists. Santiago Rebull (1829–1902) taught Diego that the basic foundation of a good painting was a good drawing. José María Velasco (1840–1912) instructed Diego on how to make his work look three dimensional.

Another artist, Félix Parra (1845–1919), introduced Diego to art that was totally different from the European pieces he was accustomed to studying. Before Spain invaded Mexico in the 1500s, the native Mexican people had produced a wealth of artwork. For example, the Olmecs, who had flourished around Mexico's Gulf Coast between 1200 and 400 B.C., had made huge stone sculptures as well as small carvings. Mayans had lived in southern Mexico from about A.D. 250 to 850 and had built pyramids and temples decorated with bright murals. The Aztecs were artists, too. They had crafted large sculptures to adorn their buildings. In addition, they had fashioned artwork from metal and clay. Unfortunately, much of the art that had been made by these and other early Mexican civilizations had been lost, destroyed, or ignored when the Spaniards conquered Mexico. When Diego attended San Carlos Academy, Félix Parra was rediscovering pre-Conquest works of art. He explained their beauty and meaning to Diego, who also began to appreciate the work.[9]

As an adult, Diego recalled one more teacher who greatly influenced him—José Guadalupe Posada (1852–1913). Though Posada was not on the San Carlos teaching staff, Diego later called him the

MEXICO

Tijuana

Hermosillo

Monterrey

La Paz

GULF OF MEXICO

Guanajuato
Mexico City • Chapingo
Veracruz
Cuernavaca
Acapulco

Yucatán Peninsula

Isthmus of Tehuantepec

Diego Rivera painted in many cities in Mexico. His art celebrated his country's heritage.

greatest of all his instructors.[10] Posada was a commercial artist who engraved flat pieces of metal with scenes of life in Mexico. Many of Posada's engravings showed ordinary people working or celebrating a holiday. Some of Posada's art expressed his opinion about current events in Mexican politics. Quite often Posada put a *calavera* in his art. A calavera is a skeleton, and it is a symbol of the Mexican holiday "The Day of the Dead." This unique holiday combines ancient traditions with religious beliefs to honor peoples' ancestors. Posada had another trademark. Below many of his engravings, he etched the words to Mexican folk songs or folktales. Once the engravings were finished, Posada used the engraved plates to make prints of his work on thin paper. He sold these prints for pennies, and they became extremely popular with ordinary citizens.

Posada's shop was near San Carlos Academy, and Diego could walk by it on his way to classes. As an adult, Diego recalled standing at the shop window frequently, watching Posada work. One day, Diego said, Posada invited him inside. They talked, and Posada took a liking to the young boy. Consequently, Diego became a regular visitor, and the man and the boy often discussed politics and art.[11] When Diego later told about the conversations he had with the great folk artist, he said, "[Posada] taught me the connection between art and life; that you can't express what you don't feel."[12]

Some scholars do not believe that Diego really knew Posada. To support their opinions, they note that throughout his life Diego frequently mentioned Rebull, Velasco, and Parra as important teachers. However, he never talked of Posada as his teacher until later in his life.[13]

Whether or not Diego actually met Posada, he no doubt saw Posada's work. Posada engraved more than fifteen thousand plates during his lifetime, and Diego must have come into contact with some of them. He may have even been touched by Posada's respectful portrayal of Mexico's everyday citizens.

When he was not at school, Diego himself could often be found among the people. Sometimes he fished with other children on the banks of a canal near San Carlos Academy. Other times he watched indigenous men in baggy white pants and women in embroidered blouses paddle boats of flowers and produce through the canal to the city markets.[14] In time, Diego's memories of these everyday Mexicans would find their way into his art.

As a young student though, Diego's artistic interests were colored by European thought and technique. When the great Mexican artist, Dr. Atl (1875–1964), returned from Europe in 1902, he was an inspiration to the students at San Carlos Academy. Atl reinforced

Diego's beliefs that true artistic study must be done on the other side of the Atlantic.[15] So Diego's dreams became firmly set on Europe. Someday, Diego hoped, he could go there to study the artistic masterpieces from history and be taught by the famous artists of the day.[16]

In the meantime, Diego continued his studies at San Carlos, painting both out-of-doors and in a studio.[17] He was already a good landscape painter and now tackled portrait painting. One of Diego's first portraits was of his mother. When María Rivera saw it, she burst into tears and called it ugly.[18] Perhaps her reaction was overly critical, though, for Diego would grow up to become one of Mexico's greatest portrait painters. However, at the time, Diego also was dissatisfied with his work. His colors did not seem realistic, and his paintings never looked quite as good as his sketches.[19] Yet he continued painting and even sold a canvas here and there. By 1904, the eighteen-year-old's reputation as a promising artist had made its way to Teodoro A. Dehesa, the governor of the state of Veracruz. Veracruz lay along Mexico's Gulf Coast, and its capitol city was also named Veracruz.

Governor Dehesa was known for giving artists financial aid. After reviewing Diego's work, he offered him a scholarship to study in Europe. The scholarship had two conditions. First, Diego must send Dehesa one painting every six months to demonstrate his progress. This condition would be easy to meet. The second condition presented more of a challenge: Diego had to raise his own travel money to Europe. Determined to see his dream come true, Diego went to work. A collection of his paintings was shown in 1906 at another San Carlos exhibit.[20] To his delight, enough pictures were sold to pay for his passage across the ocean.

Diego was going to Europe!

STUDIES ABROAD

Rivera arrived in Madrid, Spain, in January 1907. Although he was only twenty years old, the young man stood over six feet tall and weighed close to three hundred pounds. He sported a thin mustache and a short curly beard, and his dark hair frequently looked as if it had been combed into place but was slowly rebelling. Perhaps Rivera's most interesting feature was his large dark eyes. At times they were tender and sensitive but at other times they looked intellectual and questioning.

In Spain, Rivera enrolled in art classes at the Academy of Madrid. His teacher was a famous Spanish artist named Eduardo Chicharro (1676–1949). When he was not painting or attending a class, Rivera frequently visited Madrid's famous Prado Museum to sketch the paintings there. During his few free moments, he sent letters to his father and postcards to his sister, which he decorated with sketches of Spain. But Rivera had little leisure time. He threw himself into his work, sometimes painting from dawn until midnight.

When his mother suggested she come for a visit, Rivera panicked. He did not want to interrupt his studies and his painting to host her. So he wrote her a letter, asking that she wait a few months before coming to Europe. "I can say without exaggeration," he explained, "I study and paint from the time I get up until I go to bed."[1] With hurt feelings, María Rivera postponed her trip.[2] But Rivera had not been lying. His entire life was devoted to painting and study, with the exception of the small amount of time that he squeezed in for socializing.

Many nights, after finishing work, Rivera visited cafes where other artists gathered. He made friends with painters and writers who enjoyed talking about new ideas regarding art, literature, and politics. Several of his friends were socialists. Socialists believe in public ownership of a country's assets for the good of all the people. There are many different kinds of socialism, but in general, socialists believe that each member of a society should have a fair share of work, power, and wealth.

Conversations about politics inspired Rivera to read more about the topic. Rivera later reported that at that time he became interested in the philosophies of a German man named Karl Marx.[3] Marx is often thought of as the founder of a kind of socialism called communism. Marx believed that most societies were divided into two groups of people: the working class and the ruling class. People of the working class labor in a country's factories and fields, producing goods that everyone uses. These people, Marx said, are often overworked and underpaid. The ruling class consists of the wealthy business owners who employ the workers. The ruling class stays wealthy by paying their employees poorly. According to Marx, conflict between the two groups always arises because the ruling class takes advantage of the working class. To avoid this conflict, Marx said, a society's wealth and power should be divided fairly among everyone.

Although interesting to him, politics were still secondary to Rivera's art. He worked hard and constantly, and faithfully sent paintings to Dehesa every six months. Chicharro once sent Dehesa a report describing Rivera as a tireless worker and an astonishingly talented artist. This pleased Dehesa, and he helped spread Rivera's artistic reputation throughout Mexico. Rivera, however, was not as enthusiastic.

Rivera in Spain, about 1907

Later he would say that his art studies in Spain had not helped him much. He described the paintings he did there as worthless.[4] At the time, his work frustrated him. Rivera's dissatisfaction with his art may have been aggravated by exhaustion. Between working and socializing, he left little time for sleep. Exhaustion may also have been the reason why Rivera sometimes imagined he was suffering from health problems which did not exist.[5]

In the spring of 1909, Rivera left Madrid to tour Europe. He went to Paris first, where he found a room in a small hotel. As he had in Madrid, Rivera attended lectures and exhibitions. He also studied paintings that hung in Paris's museums. One of these museums, the Louvre, is among the most famous art museums in the world. Its collection includes great paintings from history such as Leonardo Da Vinci's (1452–1519) "Mona Lisa." The Louvre sits beside the Seine, a river that also flows by the Eiffel Tower, the Cathedral of Notre Dame, and other Paris landmarks. Many artists frequently gathered along the Seine River to paint, and Rivera often joined them. One painting he created during this time was called "Notre Dame Cathedral Behind the Fog."

In Paris, Rivera first encountered the work of the French painter, Paul Cézanne (1839–1906). Years later, Rivera told the following story about the first Cézanne painting he ever saw. One day as he was walking past an art shop, a Cézanne canvas displayed in the window caught his eye. He stopped to look at it, and before he knew it, an hour had passed. After another hour, the shop owner replaced the painting with another Cézanne for Rivera to view. From the sidewalk, Rivera studied this painting. Hours again passed, and the owner set out a third canvas for Rivera. At closing time, the owner removed several Cézannes from his walls and placed them on the floor where Rivera could look at them through the window. Leaving his shop lights on, the owner went home. Rivera tells of standing there for hours, so mesmerized by the paintings that he barely noticed when it began to rain. By the time he went home, he was soaked. At home, Rivera became feverish and delirious.[6] While he was sick, Rivera reported, he saw one Cézanne after another pass in front of him, even imaging some "Cézannes which Cézanne had never painted."[7]

That summer, Rivera left Paris for Brussels, Belguim. There he ran into a friend who introduced him to a Russian artist named Angeline Beloff. Rivera and Beloff traveled from Brussels to London, England, and explored the city together. They visited London's industrial neighborhoods and saw factories near the rundown housing where the workers lived. As Rivera watched these people rummage through garbage for food, he said he began to see a new reason for painting: "to produce true and complete

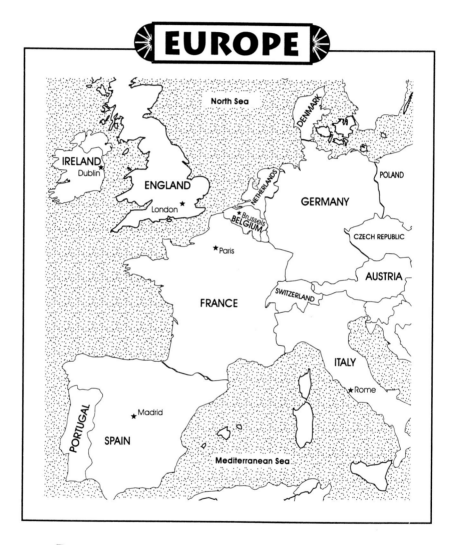

EUROPE

North Sea

IRELAND
Dublin ★

ENGLAND
★ London

NETHERLANDS

DENMARK

POLAND

GERMANY

★ Brussels
BELGIUM

★ Paris

CZECH REPUBLIC

AUSTRIA

SWITZERLAND

FRANCE

ITALY

★ Rome

PORTUGAL

★ Madrid

SPAIN

Mediterranean Sea

Rivera spent several years studying and painting in cities all across Europe.

pictures of the life of the toiling masses."[8] Yet it would be several more years before Rivera would fulfill this dream.

In the meantime, Rivera toured London's museums. At one, he saw a collection of art that had been made by Mexican artists long before Spaniards arrived in the land. The pieces fascinated him. They also touched a nerve, and Rivera returned to Paris filled with homesickness.[9] He wrote Dehesa asking permission to visit Mexico. The year was special, as 1910 marked Mexico's one-hundred-year anniversary of independence from Spain. Dehesa granted Rivera's request, telling him to bring several of his paintings for an art exhibit that would be held in Rivera's old school, the San Carlos Academy. Rivera went to work with Beloff beside him, for the two had fallen in love.[10]

It was September 1910 when Rivera started for home. He and Beloff had agreed to let time test their affection: If they were still in love when Rivera returned, they would live together. After telling Beloff good-bye, Rivera sailed for Mexico.

Perhaps it was fate that brought Rivera home in 1910. President Díaz's rule was at its most repressive, and he was now was using military force to stay in power. But opposition groups had grown in number, strength, and boldness. Most had been waiting for the right moment to revolt against Díaz. Ironically, this moment turned out to be the same one Rivera had chosen to return.

The San Carlos art show opened in November with a speech by President Díaz's wife. The exhibit was a prestigious social event, and the city's rich and privileged citizens flocked to it. Most of Rivera's paintings were sold, and several were purchased by Mrs. Díaz herself. Almost simultaneously, Mexico's bloodiest civil war broke out. It would last ten years and be called the Mexican Revolution. The revolution was fought in every major city of the nation. Eventually, it would claim the lives of over a million people. Of course, in 1910, no one knew the revolt would take on such huge dimensions. At the time, the immediate goal of the rebels was to force President Díaz from power and institute democratic elections. A man named Pancho Villa led revolutionaries in northern Mexico. In the south, Emiliano Zapata marshalled a rebel army in the state of Morelos.

Zapata had become a spokesperson for the poor and the landless of Morelos. These people respected Zapata, whom they saw as one of them. Several joined him and created a small but enthusiastic revolutionary army. Zapata led this army through the Morelos countryside, taking over haciendas and returning the land to the workers. To the poor, Emiliano Zapata became a liberator.

When the San Carlos art exhibition closed, Rivera

has said, he traveled to Morelos to see the revolution firsthand. Here, he said, the bravery of Zapata and his followers made a lifelong impression on him. Indeed, Rivera would one day see Zapata's revolts as an example of the class rebellion Karl Marx's theory predicted. For Rivera, Zapata became a symbol of an ordinary person's struggle against an oppressive ruling class.[11] As such, Zapata became the most frequently painted person in Rivera's murals.[12]

However, Rivera was not painting Zapata now. He later said that he was taking secret messages to rebel leaders in Morelos. He claimed to have been so busy doing this that he had no time to paint. Later, scholars questioned whether Rivera had really been involved in any revolutionary activities.[13] Either way, Rivera was still eager to return to Europe to further his art education.[14] With money he earned from the San Carlos exhibit, he boarded a ship to Europe, determined to improve his artistic skills. Rivera arrived in Paris in 1911.[15] An art community that would influence him for nearly a decade was waiting for him there. So was Angeline Beloff.

CHAPTER FOUR

CUBISM, WAR, AND MAYANS

Rivera and Beloff moved into a small studio in Montparnasse, a Paris neighborhood filled with artists from all over the world. There, Rivera spent his days painting. Sometimes Rivera traveled with a few artist friends to other European cities to visit museums and to paint. To save money on these journeys, the friends often huddled together in a single apartment for the length of their stay. During one of these forays, Rivera and his friends awoke in the middle of the night to find their apartment on fire. Rivera jumped from his bed, grabbed as many canvases as he could, and dashed out of the building. Although he had succeeded in saving his treasures, he soon discovered he had forgotten something else of importance—his trousers![1]

Between his travels around Europe, Rivera stayed in Paris. No matter where he was, he immersed himself in painting and the study of art. He also enjoyed discussing philosophy and politics with friends. He was a regular visitor to neighborhood cafes or other places where painters, writers, and philosophers gathered. Rivera would stay for hours, discussing new ideas or entertaining people with colorful stories.

From time to time, Rivera exhibited his paintings with the work of other artists. But few people seemed to notice his art. Then, in 1913, Rivera tried a new style of painting called cubism. Cubism is a kind of abstract art in which the subject of the painting looks as if it has been chopped up and reassembled haphazardly. In many ways, a cubist picture resembles a jigsaw puzzle that has been put together wrong. Next to bits of recognizable pieces are sharp lines and geometric shapes that cut across the picture. Sometimes a cubist painting shows the same object from several different viewpoints. In a 1913 art show in Paris, two of Rivera's early cubist paintings were exhibited. Interestingly, one critic who viewed them commented that Rivera's paintings were beautiful and looked a little like mural paintings.[2] At the time, the comment went unnoticed, for Rivera was not yet interested in painting murals. Now he was hooked on cubism. For the next four years, Rivera painted picture after picture, trying on variations of cubism as one might try on clothing. While he searched for a style all his own, he imitated the leading cubist artists of the time. One was Pablo Picasso (1881–1973), a man still remembered as a great artist.

Although he was not yet forty years old, Picasso was already hugely admired by the painters in Montparnasse. When Rivera's friends invited him to meet Picasso, Rivera was thrilled—and nervous.[3] He need not have been. Rivera and Picasso quickly became friends, and soon Picasso was visiting Rivera's studio and praising his work. Rivera's first solo exhibit in Paris was held soon afterwards. Unfortunately, the art critics had little to say about the show. This was partially because many of them simply did not like cubism. One in particular stated that Rivera's earlier work was much better, and that he hoped Rivera would return to a more conventional painting style.[4] In spite of disapproving critics, Rivera continued to experiment with cubism.

In 1914, Europe became enmeshed in World War I, a four-year war that claimed the lives of nearly 10 million soldiers. World War I began when an Austrian prince was murdered in Sarajevo, a city in a country called Austria-Hungary. Austria-Hungary accused the government of Serbia of the assassination. This accusation fanned the flames of an old conflict between these two countries. Within a month, Austria-Hungary had declared war on Serbia. Quickly, Russia, France, and England jumped to Serbia's defense. It was not long before other European countries were choosing sides in the battle. By the fall of 1914, Serbia, England, France, and Russia (called the Allies) were at war against Austria-Hungary and Germany (called the Central Powers). The majority of the fighting occurred along the borders of Germany, Austria-Hungary, Russia, and France.

The outbreak of World War I had a great impact on the artists in Paris. Many were from one of the battling countries, and they returned to their homes to fight. Other artists left Paris, and Rivera was among them. He and Beloff traveled to Spain, where they would stay until the spring of 1915. Spain was a neutral country and did not become involved in the war. But the magnitude of World War I made its sorrows and hardships nearly inescapable. To the majority of Europeans, it was a subject of daily concern. Most had husbands, sons, or brothers fighting and dying on the front lines. In this atmosphere, art was forgotten and artists sold little. Consequently, Rivera and Beloff were extremely poor. To make matters worse, the Mexican Revolution had brought an end to Rivera's scholarship money from the government.

By April 1915, Rivera was back in Paris living on thin soups. Even so, he never took another job, and he never stopped painting.

As he worked, Rivera developed a distinctive style. While other cubist artists painted in muted tones, Rivera used bright, vibrant colors. In addition, Rivera mixed sand into his paint to add texture to his work. Mexican motifs kept creeping onto his canvases. In 1915, Rivera painted a picture that foreshadowed his future as an artist of the Mexican people. This picture was a cubist painting called "Zapatista Landscape." More than any other work he had painted, this picture was about Rivera's constantly growing sympathy for the poor people of Mexico. In clear, bold colors, Rivera painted pieces of a *serape* (shawl) and a *sombrero* (hat) like the one worn by the Mexican folk hero, Emiliano Zapata. Nearby were a rifle and cartridge belt, representing revolution. Behind these elements, Rivera painted the mountains that surround Mexico City. In addition, Rivera painted an interesting scrap of paper in the bottom right hand corner of his canvas. Looking as if it had been nailed to the picture, this note card was a common feature in Mexican folk paintings. In folk paintings, the note card told the name of the artist or the event that had inspired the painting. Even though Rivera left his note card blank, its presence was a proclamation of his Mexican heritage. "Zapatista Landscape" was seen as a unique canvas in a sea of similar paintings then being created by other artists. According to one critic, Rivera "follows his own road. . . . Between a painting by Rivera and one by Picasso there is as much distance as between a mountain and a forest."[5]

Actually, distance was growing in the two artists' friendship as well. Frequent visits to each others' studios resulted in hours of philosophical discussions about art and politics. Their opinions, however, frequently clashed. Furthermore, Rivera sometimes became angry at Picasso's habit of roaming freely around his studio, looking over Rivera's latest works.[6] "One of these days," Rivera told a friend, "either I'll chuck [Picasso] out or I'll shove off to Mexico."[7] Although the friendship between the artists ended, Rivera would always admire Picasso's talent. Of him, he once said, "I have never believed in God, but I believe in Picasso."[8]

By 1916, Rivera was considered a major cubist painter. That same year, Rivera's works were exhibited in the United States for the first time. Many of his paintings were shown in a New York City show next to the art of Cézanne, Picasso, and Vincent Van Gogh (1853–1890). In October, a large collection of Rivera's work was again shown in New York City with several pieces of Aztec art. As Rivera built his reputation as an artist, Beloff painted pieces that would pay the rent and buy the groceries. The two had never married,

Rivera painted this cubist rendition of the Mexican folk hero
Emiliano Zapata, "Zapatista Landscape," in 1915.

but continued to live together. In 1916, Beloff gave birth to a son they named Diego. Because Rivera refused to let the infant keep him from his work, Beloff assumed full responsibility for little Diego.[9] As she cared for the baby, a great change was taking place in her homeland.

For centuries, Russia had been ruled by emperors called czars. Czars were dictators who lived in luxury while the majority of the Russian people nearly starved. During the early years of the twentieth century, thousands of Russians labored in harsh conditions in factories, fields, and mines. In 1905, rebellion swept the nation as various groups organized to overthrow the czar. One political uprising followed another, but none were entirely successful. When Germany invaded Russia in 1914, the rebellions stopped and Russians turned their attention to defending their borders.

Yet war only made the Russian people poorer. Worse still, the Russian army was suffering defeat after defeat. Again, people became angry at the government. Again, revolutionaries struck out. In 1917, a man named Vladimir Lenin led thousands of Russian workers in a bloody takeover of the Russian government. His assistant was Leon Trotsky. Both Lenin and Trotsky were communists. Once Lenin became the ruler of Russia, he began implementing Karl Marx's ideas about how a society should be organized. He gave land to poor farmers and transferred factory ownership to the workers.

Rivera watched the 1917 Russian Revolution with excitement. He was happy to see Lenin come to power, feeling that armed rebellion was the only way poor people anywhere could throw off the chains of their oppressors.[10] Beloff felt differently. She was a pacifist, and therefore was against war for any reason.

Unfortunately, being a pacifist could not keep tragedy from Beloff's door. Heating fuel and food were in short supply, and when they were available, they were costly. So Rivera, Beloff, and Diego, Jr., lived in constant cold and hunger. Then came the greatest hardship of all—in the fall of 1918, little Diego became sick and died. He was only two years old.

While Beloff mourned the loss of their son, Rivera sought solace in his art and politics. Although World War I was finally ending, the Mexican Revolution was still being fought. Since Díaz had been thrown from power, three different men had ruled Mexico. The current leader, Venustiano Carranza, was doing little to help the poor. In many ways, the Mexican people were in the same situation the Russian people had been in before the Russian Revolution. Perhaps, Rivera thought, art could be a useful tool in Mexico's revolution.[11] Maybe art could show ordinary citizens how important they were to their nation. Rivera felt that once workers understood their value, they would understand their power. This power might give them courage to revolt against unfair rulers.[12] Now Rivera's ideas about art helping the ordinary person began to take a clearer shape.

Rivera realized that art that would inspire the common citizen could not be tucked away in elegant art galleries or in the homes of rich people. Workers and farmers never saw art in these places. Art with a social message for ordinary people would have to be displayed in places where it would be seen—in post offices, schools, railroad stations, and other public buildings.[13] Rivera sensed something else. Art for the common person would have to be technically superior and exciting to look at.[14]

These thoughts made Rivera question cubism. Cubism was so abstract that most people had difficulty understanding it. It seemed to him that the only people who truly understood cubist paintings were formally educated artists. This made the style useless to everyday citizens.[15] Because of his new focus on using art for the people, cubism became useless to Rivera, as well. He later said:

> I stopped painting in the cubist manner because of the war, the Russian Revolution, and my belief in the need for a popular and socialized art. It had to be a functional art, related to the world and to the times, and had to serve to help the masses to a better social organization.[16]

During the past four years, Rivera had produced more than two hundred cubist paintings and become one of the style's most original artists. Years later, he would recognize that he used cubist principles in all of his future paintings. He even called cubism "the most important development in art since the Renaissance."[17] But at the time, Rivera turned away from it.

At about this time, Rivera met another Mexican artist who was in Paris. David Alfaro Siqueiros (1898–1974) had actually fought in the Mexican Revolution. He entertained Rivera for hours with stories about his experiences. Siqueiros also told Rivera about the political movement brewing among Mexico's artists. Many, he said, were socialists who wanted to use art to express their political ideas. This excited Rivera, since it seemed to echo his own thoughts.[18]

In 1920, Alvaro Obregón became the president of Mexico. His rise to power brought an end to the revolution, and Obregón set out to rebuild Mexico. He gave land to the poor, supported labor reform, and wanted to increase educational opportunities for the average Mexican. Most important to Rivera, though, Obregón selected a man named José Vasconcelos to head up the nation's Department of Education. As minister of Education, Vasconcelos ordered the building of new schools and public libraries all across the country. He made art a required subject in school for all children. He even created opportunities for

interested adults to take art classes from formally educated artists. This last program brought schooled artists into close contact with people who had had no
formal art training. Many of these people, though,
were artists in another sense.

Ordinary Mexicans had always created art. But
instead of painting pictures for art galleries, their
artistic talents were used to beautify the objects they
used every day. For example, the clothing many Mexicans wore was handwoven and decorated with unique
designs. Another popular form of folk art was the
ex-voto. An ex-voto was a small oil painting on a
piece of tin. The painting was always religious, and
most often it showed how a saint helped someone in
need. Ex-votos were placed on church altars as a
thank-you for divine assistance. In addition, mural
painting had been popular throughout Mexico's history.
Ancient Mayan artists had painted pictures on the
walls of their buildings, illustrating their lives and cus-
toms. Centuries later, the walls of Catholic churches
were decorated with religious murals. In Rivera's
youth, humorous paintings or picturesque landscapes
were often painted on the sides of small taverns called
pulquerías.

Actually, murals were found not only in Mexico,
but all over the world and throughout history. The earliest humans had painted their caves with stories about
their lives. Later civilizations decorated tombs and

temples with murals. One of the greatest mural painters of all time was the Italian artist, Michelangelo
(1475–1564). Among Michelangelo's most famous
murals are the paintings he created on the ceiling of
the Sistine Chapel in the Vatican. In beautiful detail,
Michelangelo illustrated nine stories from the Bible,
including God creating the world, Adam and Eve, and
Noah and the flood.

When Rivera sold a portrait for a large profit, he
filled his knapsack with brushes and paint and traveled
to Italy. For seventeen months, he wandered through
the country studying art. A large portion of this time
was spent examining Michelangelo's paintings at the
Sistine Chapel. Rivera mentally dissected the work,
then sketched the murals over and over again.
Michelangelo left an indelible imprint on Rivera, much
as Picasso had. Rivera learned important technical
lessons from this study. Michelangelo's murals also
demonstrated to Rivera the power of this art form.
Rivera saw murals as an effective tool for communi-
cating with the common person. Murals could be
moving, exciting, and meaningful.[19] By 1921, Rivera
had accumulated over three hundred sketches of
Michelangelo's work. In addition, he had developed a
burning desire to return to Mexico.[20] In June, Rivera
told Beloff good-bye with a promise to send for her
when he was able. She was soon forgotten.

Rivera described his 1921 arrival home as a

rebirth. He said the colors of Mexico energized him: The bright hues seemed brighter and full of light, and the dark tones rich and deep. Rivera saw a painting everywhere he looked—in the markets, the shops, and the fields.[21] As he sketched, a new style emerged, a style Rivera said was born "in a moment, except that this birth had come after a torturous pregnancy of thirty-five years."[22]

In the meantime, Beloff sent Rivera countless letters asking him to send for her. He rarely answered. Exciting events in the art community had captured his attention. The Mexican artists that David Alfaro Siqueiros had told Rivera about were forming an artists' union. It was called the Syndicate of Technical Workers, Painters, and Sculptors and was committed to creating art for everyone in Mexican society. In a statement of its beliefs, the Syndicate said it wanted to liberate the oppressed by creating art for and about them. Most of the union's artists also wanted their work to reflect their Mexican heritage and traditions. Rivera joined the Syndicate and soon was helping to write its newsletter. Many of its articles explained and advocated communist beliefs.

In November, Vasconcelos invited Rivera on a trip to the Yucatán Peninsula. The Yucatán was the land of the Mayans. Since prehistoric time, the Mayans had lived in this region and produced magnificent paintings, pottery, and sculptures. They had developed a sophisticated understanding of architecture, astronomy, and mathematics. In addition, the Mayans were among the first people in the Western Hemisphere to develop a written language. Their writing was based on various symbols that represented sounds or ideas. When several of the symbols were drawn next to each other, they told a story. This kind of writing system is called hieroglyphics.

Rivera accepted Vasconcelos's invitation. At the Yucatán, he toured the centuries-old ruins of a great Mayan city called Chichén Itzá. There he saw pyramids, temples, and shrines. But Rivera was most impressed by the murals that decorated the buildings. He spent hours simply gazing at them. Mayans who had lived and died centuries before Rivera was born were now speaking to him through their art—and filling him with inspiration.

MURALS FOR
THE PEOPLE

Upon their return to Mexico City, Vasconcelos asked Rivera to paint at the National Preparatory School, a high school in Mexico City for exceptionally bright students. Other artists were already experimenting with mural painting there.[1] Most of the murals they were creating were frescoes. A fresco is a picture painted directly onto a plastered wall while the plaster is still wet. As the paint and plaster dry together, the paint becomes permanently bound to the plaster.

Rivera went to work on a mural of his own. When

he completed it in 1922, he was unhappy with the results. He felt that it looked too much like the murals he had seen in Europe. He also thought it was too symbolic for most people to understand.[2] Critics later agreed with his assessment.[3] Even though Rivera had not yet perfected the artistic style for which he would become famous, one thing was certain—he had found his form.

He had also found a new love. While working at the Preparatory School, Rivera met a woman named Guadalupe Marín. Marín was tall and slim with auburn hair, light brown skin, and green eyes. Rivera sketched and painted Marín, and her portrait appeared in several of his later works. The two fell in love and were married in a church ceremony in 1922.[4]

As always, though, art was Rivera's first love, and now he was smitten with mural making. However, painting walls was not very profitable. So while he worked on the mural, Rivera squeezed in time to paint canvases, which he sold quite easily. But he spent his wages almost as quickly as he earned them. He had recently joined the Communist party of Mexico and frequently made generous donations to it. Rivera also spent a large portion of his earnings on the pre-Conquest indigenous sculptures that he had begun collecting. Marín later reported, "whatever money Diego made, he spent on his idols or donated to the [Communist party]. He never thought of any practical ways to spend his money. Such prosaic things as food, clothing, or the rent were his last considerations."[5]

Marín was right. Rivera did not seem worried about these aspects of everyday life. His art overshadowed all else. In 1922, he went on another trip sponsored by Vasconcelos. This time Rivera journeyed to the Isthmus of Tehuantepec, an area of Mexico where the native culture was still very much alive. There Rivera saw men and women who looked and dressed much as their ancestors had before the Spaniards arrived. Rivera filled notebook after notebook with sketches of them. Although he did not know it then, Rivera would use these sketches in his paintings for the rest of his life.

In 1923, Rivera began a new mural project commissioned by Vasconcelos. This time he was working on the walls at the Ministry of Education building. This job was one more part of Vasconcelos's ambitious plan to expose the general public to art. Rivera was one of many artists Vasconcelos had hired to paint in buildings all over Mexico City. Most of the artists belonged to the Syndicate. To encourage freedom of artistic expression, the artists were told they could paint whatever they chose. They were paid a daily wage and had no time limit for completing their work. These conditions were a great liberation for the artists. They could express their ideas freely and experiment with various artistic techniques without worrying about earning a living. Years later, experts would label this time period in Mexican art the "Mexican Renaissance." Three muralists emerged from the era as international stars: Diego Rivera, David Alfaro Siqueiros, and José Clemente Orozco (1883–1949). One day this trio would be known worldwide as Mexico's *"Los tres grandes"*("the big three") artists.[6] Right now, each was busy painting murals for Vasconcelos.

Not everyone liked Vasconcelos's mural program. Because the Syndicate artists often glorified poor people and criticized the rich, wealthy people were frequently offended by the artists' paintings. Many of these wealthy citizens were a powerful force in the Mexican government, and when particular murals angered them, they protested to Vasconcelos. Some people said the artists were ruining public buildings.[7] Other people disliked the way some artists painted Mexicans. For example, the people in Rivera's frescoes often had dark skin and broad noses and looked very different from the light-skinned Europeans typically seen in famous artwork.[8] Some Mexicans found this new style too different for their tastes. As one man gazed upon a Rivera mural, he commented about the woman in it. "How would you like to be married to a woman that looked like that?" he asked his companion. Overhearing him, Rivera replied, "Young man, neither would you want to marry a pyramid, but a pyramid is also art."[9] A few unhappy Mexicans even

Diego Rivera at work

destroyed murals they disliked. Adding fuel to the fire, newspapers criticized the artists. In spite of the criticism, Vasconcelos continued hiring artists, and some painters climbed onto their scaffolds armed with pistols to discourage vandals.

As Rivera worked at the Ministry of Education, one of his paintings caused an even larger controversy. This painting showed tired miners emerging from a mine. Below the picture, Rivera had copied a poem that encouraged the workers to make knives from the metal they dug and take over the mines. When a few people objected to the poem, Vasconcelos asked Rivera to remove it. But Syndicate artists supported Rivera's right to free expression, and told him to leave the poem as it was. Rivera compromised. He chipped the poem from the wall and replaced it with a less rebellious poem.[10] Although Rivera weathered this storm, many people continued to demand an end to Vasconcelos's mural program. Finally, Vasconcelos gave in to them. He stopped commissioning murals and fired many of the artists who were already working. Then, in 1924, he himself resigned as the minister of Education.

As scaffolds around the city were dismantled, Rivera argued with the Syndicate about how to handle the situation. In the face of the disagreement, he left the union. Some artists thought that Rivera's resignation came at a convenient time—for him. They claimed that when Rivera saw Syndicate artists being fired, he knew his own painting jobs were in jeopardy. They said he started the argument so he would have a reason to resign from the union, knowing he would probably keep his own mural commissions if he were not a Syndicate member. Siqueiros called Rivera an opportunist. Whether or not the charges were true, Rivera was the lone survivor of the government sweep to rid the city of muralists.[11] As other artists disappeared from public buildings, Rivera continued his work at the Ministry of Education.

That same year, Marín gave birth to a daughter, who was named Lupe. Marín and Rivera would later have a second child, Ruth. Predictably, Rivera did not see his family much, for he was busy painting. When involved in a project, he often worked eighteen hours a day, seven days a week. He rarely stopped for a meal, and instead snacked on food that was brought to him. Marín complained that Rivera did not even stop to bathe.[12] As usual, Rivera's art came before all else.

In November 1924, Rivera took time from his Ministry of Education work to paint murals at an agricultural college in Chapingo, Mexico. The murals he painted there are considered to be among Rivera's best.[13] Marín served as his model for several of the female nudes in the murals that represented nature. In another section of the frescoes, Rivera attempted to express his belief that societies, like plants, grow and change. In one panel, a seedling grows into a flower. Nearby, poor farmers revolt against rich landowners. A third scene connects nature with society. It shows the revolutionary leader, Emiliano Zapata, buried in the earth with blood flowing from his body and fertilizing the soil. Rivera occasionally left his work at Chapingo to continue his murals at the Ministry of Education.

Then, as he finished his murals at Chapingo, Rivera was invited to Moscow to represent Mexico's Communist party at the tenth-anniversary celebration of the Russian Revolution. His 1927 journey was well timed. Rivera had not been a faithful husband, and Marín would not accept such behavior. At one gathering, she shouted at Rivera about an affair he had once had with a party guest. Then she tore up some of his drawings and physically attacked the woman.[14] In the face of Marín's anger, Rivera welcomed a chance to get away.[15]

After six months in Russia, Rivera came back to Mexico toting hundreds of drawings and paintings he had made of Russian parades, speeches, and everyday life. He then returned to the Ministry of Education to complete the frescoes he had begun there four years earlier. When he finally finished the work in 1928, Rivera had painted 124 murals in the three-story, two-block-long building. Added together, these paintings covered over seventeen thousand square feet. Had Rivera painted the same area in pictures only one foot high, they would have stretched for three miles!

This massive work was important for many reasons. First, in spite of the end to Vasconcelos's mural program, the enormous fresco project signified the firm establishment of murals in twentieth-century Mexican art. Second, the subject matter of Rivera's frescoes was socially significant. His murals were really a picture book of all things Mexican. Rivera had painted Mexicans mining, farming, and weaving. (In one panel he painted himself as an architect to symbolize his role as the master planner of the entire project.) Some of the frescoes showed Mexicans celebrating religious holidays. Others showed them participating in folk festivals. Rivera painted Mexican markets and landscapes. As one writer stated, future historians could look at these paintings and be able to "reconstruct a rich and varied picture of the Mexican land, its people, their labors, festivals, [and] ways of living."[16] Taken as a whole, Rivera's work dignified native Mexican culture.

Finally, the Ministry of Education murals were significant in terms of the future political content of Rivera's mural art. Several of the panels incorporated Rivera's political views. In one painting, for example, a rebel handed out guns to a crowd of revolutionaries. In another, Rivera painted the portraits of people who had died in the Mexican Revolution, including Emiliano Zapata. These paintings were among the first murals that expressed Rivera's communist beliefs. Many more would follow.

As Rivera completed his Ministry of Education work, Marín left him, taking their two daughters. There were others, too, who did not relish his company. But while some disliked the man personally, many people respected his artistic talent. Wherever he worked, people gathered to watch. One onlooker said that although Rivera was heavy and cumbersome he had "sensitive . . . slender fingers [that were as] flexible as the limbs of a dancer."[17]

Another of Rivera's admirers was a young woman named Frida Kahlo. Kahlo had been born in 1907 in Coyoacán, Mexico. She had suffered from polio as a child, and the disease had permanently crippled her right leg. But Kahlo was a bright young girl, and she was attending the National Preparatory School at the same time Rivera was there painting his first murals. Kahlo was a mischievous child, and stories about her pranks abound. One tale tells of her soaping the steps near Rivera, hoping to make him slip and fall. Another reports that she teased Guadalupe Marín when Marín came to visit Rivera. When Rivera finished his work at the school, Kahlo disappeared from his life—for a while.

In 1925, Kahlo was in a horrible streetcar accident

that nearly killed her. A metal handrail pierced her body, breaking her back and pelvis. For a long time Kahlo stayed in bed, wrapped in various splints and casts. To occupy herself, she painted. Although she eventually recovered her mobility, she would live much of her life in pain.

Thinking of ways she could earn a living, Kahlo turned to art. One day, as Rivera was painting at the Ministry of Education, she went to him with some of her work. When she introduced herself, Rivera remembered her as the imp who had teased him at the Preparatory School a few years earlier. Kahlo explained that she was seeking an honest appraisal of her artistic talent. If she was not good enough to earn a living at it, she wanted to know so she could pursue a different career. But Rivera liked her work. He also liked her and began courting her in earnest. Rivera later said that soon after they met, Kahlo became the most important thing in his life.[18]

Although Kahlo's friends could not understand her attraction to Rivera, she was definitely in love. He was also in love. In 1929, the two were married.[19] Rivera was forty-three years old and Kahlo was only twenty-two. The couple moved into an elegant house on a famous street in Mexico City called the Paseo de la Reforma. Several people came to live with them there, including Siqueiros and his wife.

That spring, Rivera became the art director at

Not long after they were married, Rivera and Kahlo posed for this photograph in Kahlo's Coyoacán home.

San Carlos Academy. His acceptance of this position angered the Communist party. President Obregón had been assassinated in 1928, and now Plutarco Calles was Mexico's president. Many of Calles's policies were directed at keeping communists out of the government. This, of course, infuriated members of the Communist party. They saw Rivera's acceptance of the San Carlos job as approval of Calles's actions. Rivera disagreed. He said he had refused an offer to be the minister of Fine Arts because of Calles's policies. But San Carlos Academy, Rivera argued, was different. It was an independent institution unrelated to the government.

Rivera's standing in Mexico's Communist party was further damaged when he accepted a job painting murals at the National Palace. Once more, the Communist party saw this as Rivera's support of the Calles government. This time the party took action. In September 1929, Rivera was declared unworthy of party membership and thrown out of Mexico's Communist party. For a while, Rivera said, he felt like he was without a home.[20] During the next two decades, he would ask to be let back into the Communist party several times, but it was not until late in his life that he was readmitted.

The pressures of the year had sapped Rivera. In the fall, he became ill and remained in bed. As Kahlo nursed him back to health, Calles increased his efforts to quiet people who disagreed with his policies.

Communists were being sent to prison, deported, and some even murdered. When Rivera's health improved, he began painting his famous frescoes above the staircase at the National Palace. Yet each day when he left for work, he did not know if he would be allowed to continue painting.[21] Finally, Rivera stopped working at the National Palace and left Mexico City.

He and Kahlo traveled to Cuernavaca, a city to the south in the state of Morelos. The United States ambassador to Mexico, Dwight Morrow, lived there. Morrow had hired Rivera to paint at the Palace of Cortés, a government building that had been erected in the sixteenth century. Rivera's frescoes were to be a gift from the United States to the Mexican people. In the historic building, Rivera painted scenes that dramatized Cuernavaca's history from Aztec times to the 1910 revolution. He showed the Spanish conquistador Hernando Cortés overseeing enslaved native Mexicans as they built the palace. He painted a hacienda owner relaxing in a hammock while peasant farmers labored in his fields. Last, but far from least, Rivera included a portrait of Emiliano Zapata in one of his panels, for it was in Morelos that this revolutionary hero had begun his fight.

As he painted, Rivera learned that Siqueiros had been thrown into jail as punishment for demonstrating against Calles. Then came the news that Rivera had been fired from San Carlos Academy. It seemed like a good time to leave Mexico.[22] He decided to travel to the United States.

RIVERA MEETS AMERICA

Many art lovers in the United States had been watching the art renaissance in Mexico unfold. Several admired the work of the revolutionary artists and were especially interested in Diego Rivera. Many of his paintings already hung in United States museums or had been in exhibitions there.

But not everyone liked Rivera's work immediately. One art patron described the first Rivera painting he owned as having faded colors and looking childishly simple. But because the picture had been a gift, he hung it in his studio. "To my surprise," he said, "I could not take my eyes off of it, and in the course of a few days, my reaction to the picture changed completely."[1] He came to view the painting as powerful, and he consequently became one of Rivera's biggest fans in the United States.[2] He, along with a few other people, wanted the artist to visit the country. Ironically, these enthusiasts were wealthy—the very people Rivera's work so often condemned. But this did not dampen his fans' zeal. They repeatedly invited Rivera to the United States. Repeatedly, he declined. Until 1930.

That year Rivera accepted an invitation to paint at the San Francisco Stock Exchange. The public announcement of Rivera's upcoming visit set off a flurry of protest. Some people felt that a United States artist should have been chosen for the job. Others criticized Rivera's communist beliefs. These objections did not stop Rivera: He saw the invitation to the United States as an opportunity to continue working without the threat of censorship.[3] Furthermore, United States' cities were filled with factories and factories were filled with machines. Rivera's love for machinery could be thoroughly indulged in the United States. Best of all, Rivera reasoned that a capitalist nation was the perfect place to sow the seeds of communism.[4] Capitalism is a political system very different from communism. Capitalists believe that a country's land and factories should be privately owned. They feel that variations in personal wealth are good for a society.

Rivera and Kahlo arrived in San Francisco in November 1930. Soon the protests against Rivera's presence stopped, and newspapers were writing colorful stories about the artist. In one he was described as a "jovial, big jowled: [man] beaming behind an ever-present cigar, his clothes bulkier than his big frame, a broad-brimmed hat . . . on his curly locks."[5] Rivera's United States hosts threw him lavish parties and even took him to a college football game. People were also captivated by Kahlo, who looked so tiny and frail next to her husband. In addition, the unique clothes Kahlo wore heightened her exotic appeal. Since marrying Rivera, she had taken to dressing in long, ruffled skirts and colorful, embroidered blouses like the clothing worn by the indigenous women of Tehuantepec. Kahlo further adorned herself with necklaces, bracelets, and earrings. Even her hair was decorated, most often worn wrapped on her head with brightly colored yarn woven through it.

For several weeks, Rivera toured San Francisco thinking about his mural. As he had in London, he saw the wealthy and the poor. He gazed at mansions, then watched unemployed people line up for a free meal. But Rivera also saw a state rich in resources. By December, he was ready to paint. First, he fashioned a huge woman that symbolized California. In her outstretched arms he painted the state's bounty. Wheat and grapes stood for agriculture. Gold miners

Rivera and Kahlo shortly after their arrival in San Francisco,
California, in 1930

and lumberjacks depicted the state's natural resources. Engineers represented what human intellect had brought to California. Rivera's work, "Allegory of California," was officially inaugurated on March 15, 1931.

Next, Rivera painted at the California School of Fine Arts. This mural's theme was the building of a modern industrial city. Rivera's painting showed many different kinds of workers, including architects, steel-workers, and artists. One section of his work showed a fresco being made, and Rivera painted himself into this portion as the mural's artist. In the painting, he was seated on a scaffold looking at his work with his back to the viewer.

By now, Rivera was becoming a sensation.[6] When the New York Museum of Modern Art gave him a one-person exhibition in 1931, it was a definite sign of his artistic success in the United States. The show featured 151 oils, pastels, watercolors, and murals from the course of Rivera's career. The art critics liked the show, which set museum attendance records when almost fifty-seven thousand people came to see Rivera's work.[7]

After the exhibit, Rivera traveled to Detroit, Michigan, where he had been hired to paint about the development of that city's industry. As he had in San Francisco, Rivera began with research. Sketching his way around Detroit, Rivera studied workshops at the Ford and Chrysler automobile factories. He visited a chemical plant and a drug manufacturer. Soon, drawings of furnaces, assembly lines, science laboratories, and the people who worked them filled his notebooks. One of the highlights of his research was a tour of Greenfield Village, a nearby museum of machines. There Rivera saw displays that traced the development of machinery from its primitive beginnings to the present day. Rivera decided that Detroit's murals would show how machinery could free society from the drudgeries of work and explain how advances in technology could help humanity.[8] In June 1932, he set to work painting on the four huge walls that surrounded a courtyard at the Detroit Institute of Arts.

By March 1933, Rivera had completed his frescoes. He had also lost over one hundred pounds. Much of his weight loss could be attributed to his fifteen-hour-a-day, seven-day-a-week schedule. One observer reported that Rivera once worked thirty-six hours straight. The artist's own dedication, the observer said, was why Rivera's assistants were willing to put in long hours, too.[9]

Rivera's finished product was divided into four themes, one for each wall. The first mural depicted the earth as the origin of all life. Its main focus was a baby nestled in what appeared to be its mother's womb. Closer inspection showed that the womb was really the bulb of a plant. The next mural explored the technologies of air and water. Airplanes, ships, and their machinery dominated this panel. The third and fourth murals were huge, intricate paintings that focused on the various industries of Detroit. In these, people of all races worked side by side producing automobiles, chemicals, and pharmaceuticals.

In one panel, Rivera had painted a picture that looked much like a Christian nativity scene. In it, a mother holds her toddler while a doctor vaccinates him. The mother is wearing a glowing hat that resembles a halo. Behind them, three scientists work at a microscope, looking somewhat like the three wise men. Finally, the barnyard animals so familiar in nativity scenes stand in the foreground of Rivera's painting waiting for vaccinations of their own. This particular panel brought disapproval from some of Detroit's clergy. They believed it was sacrilegious. When they protested, Detroit workers quickly came to Rivera's defense, saying that they liked all of the murals and did not want any of them changed. Then Edsel Ford, the son of Henry Ford and the man who had paid for the Detroit murals, became involved. When he declared that Rivera's artwork reflected the spirit of Detroit, the matter was put to rest. Today, many art critics consider Rivera's Detroit murals to be the best work he created in the United States.[10]

By now, Rivera had perfected his fresco painting techniques. He began each project by studying the wall he was to paint, carefully considering any particular

The north wall of "Detroit Industry," Rivera's mural at the Detroit Institute of Arts, shows men working at an automobile factory.

features of the space. Once he had a clear concept of how to incorporate a building's architecture into a design, Rivera made sketches of his ideas.[11] He worked on these drawings carefully because early in his art training, he had learned that a good sketch was the foundation of a good painting.[12] When Rivera was happy with his sketches, they were enlarged to the size they would appear in the fresco. These huge drawings, called cartoons, showed Rivera how his small drawings would actually look on a wall. At times, the cartoons were revised. Once they were correct, a portion of the wall was plastered. Then the appropriate parts of the cartoons were outlined on the fresh plaster.[13] Sometimes Rivera made a few more changes before actually beginning to paint, but at this stage he had to move quickly because his painting had to be finished before the plastered section dried. This gave Rivera about eight to sixteen hours to work.[14] At the end of each work day, Rivera carefully looked over his painting and made any necessary revisions. Once the plaster dried, the only way to change the fresco was by chipping the plaster from the wall and starting all over again.[15]

In March 1933, Rivera traveled to New York City to work on a mural for the RCA building. This building was owned by one of the wealthiest families in the United States, the Rockefellers. The Rockefellers had earned their fortune in the oil industry during the late

These "cartoons" were assembled for one of Rivera's murals at the Detroit Institute of Arts.

1800s. Since then, the family had given millions of dollars to the arts, education, and charities. The RCA building held the headquarters of many of the charitable foundations the Rockefellers supported.[16] It was to be decorated with artwork created by several different artists. Unfortunately, Rivera's mural at the RCA building would cause much controversy.

The project began well enough. The theme for all of the artwork in the building had already been decided before Rivera was hired. Each piece was to address the topic, "Man at the crossroads looking with hope and high vision to the choosing of a new and better future." Individual artists were told to interpret this topic however they chose. Rivera saw the "crossroads" as the differing paths of capitalism and communism. He created a sketch of his mural idea and submitted it for approval. In his sketch, a large machine symbolizing science and technology dominated the area. The empty spaces around and between the pieces of machinery were filled with portraits of workers and wealthy people. Nelson Rockefeller, the project's coordinator, approved the sketches.[17] Rockefeller's favorable opinion, however, did not last. In April, a newspaper reported that Rivera was creating a communist mural with Rockefeller's approval. The article told about a portrait of the Russian revolutionary, Vladimir Lenin, that Rivera had drawn onto the wall. Interestingly,

Lenin's portrait had not appeared in Rivera's original sketches.[18]

Critics later questioned why Rivera added Lenin to his mural. One theorized that Rivera had simply gotten carried away. He had just come from visiting factories in Detroit where people were clearly divided into two classes—managers and workers. Perhaps after witnessing this, Rivera felt it necessary to paint about the communist principles Lenin had used to change Russia. Whatever Rivera's reasons were, he was asked to paint out Lenin's face.[19] Rivera refused, saying he would rather destroy his entire mural than compromise his artistic vision.[20] Besides, said Rivera, everyone knew he was a communist when he was hired. Almost all of his work expressed his political beliefs. Rivera continued, "[No one had the] right to expect that . . . [the RCA mural] would be of a different character."[21]

But Rivera felt an even larger principle was at stake. Once an artist was hired, he believed, that artist must be free to create anything. This was both an artistic right and an obligation.[22] To illustrate his point, Rivera asked if someone who bought the Sistine Chapel had the right to destroy Michelangelo's work. Or, if a person who purchased Albert Einstein's unpublished manuscripts could burn those papers. Still, Rivera was not blind to the realities of his own situation. Sensing that the fresco might really be destroyed, Rivera secretly photographed his work.[23] Then he continued to

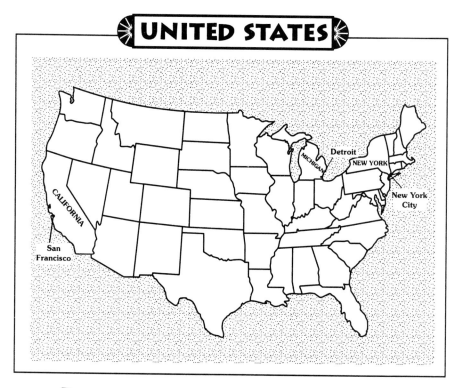

Rivera painted murals in San Francisco, Detroit, and New York City. Many can still be viewed by the public.

paint until a day in May when men suddenly surrounded him and led him from the building. Rivera was paid for his mural, then ordered to stop work immediately. His scaffolds were removed, and the wall was covered with canvas.[24]

This act set off a furor that made international news. People everywhere spoke out about the incident. Many disliked Rivera's mural and supported Rockefeller's actions. Their views were echoed by the man who wrote in a *New York Times* newspaper editorial, "I do not believe that even a noted foreign artist is entitled to abuse American standards or political thought."[25] Other people sided with Rivera. Two hundred of them demonstrated outside the RCA building, carrying signs that read, "Save Rivera's murals from Rockefeller's vandalism."[26] These protesters then marched to Rockefeller's house where police met them and ended the demonstration. Despite the support for Rivera, the mural was never finished.

The fiasco at the RCA building proved fatal to Rivera's mural-making career in the United States. Commissions he had already signed were canceled, and he received no new offers. Except one. It came from a group that shared Rivera's political views, the New Workers School in New York City. In 1933, Rivera painted twenty-one frescoes there, which he titled "Portrait of America." These panels were a series of paintings depicting various conflicts in United States history that were caused by the oppression of one group of people by another. For example, Rivera painted Native Americans being exploited by colonists, Africans being sold as slaves, and factory workers striking against intolerable working conditions.

By 1934, Rivera and Kahlo were back in Mexico. They had moved into a new house built just for them in a section of Mexico City called San Angel. The unique structure consisted of two separate buildings joined by a rooftop bridge. Each side of the house had its own living space and art studio. Soon after moving in, Rivera learned that his partially finished mural in the RCA building had been removed from the wall. He called the action "an act of cultural vandalism."[27] When he was asked to reproduce a smaller version of the mural at Mexico City's Palace of Fine Arts, he accepted. The finished painting differed a little from the original, but the basic design and central theme remained—and so did Vladimir Lenin.

Apparently, Rivera's first visit north of the border had ended in disaster. Or had it? Wherever Rivera had painted in the United States, artists had flocked to watch the master muralist work. A few were hired as his assistants and learned about fresco painting firsthand. One in particular, Ben Shahn (1898–1969), would become a well-known United States muralist.

Other artists watched from a distance. Thomas Hart Benton (1889–1975), one of the United States'

Rivera's repainted version of the RCA building fresco "Man at the Crossroads." Vladimir Lenin is the bearded man on the right who is clasping the hands of workers of different races.

most famous artists of the 1920s and 1930s, had observed Rivera and other Mexican muralists for many years. Benton later said that their "concern with publicly significant meanings and with the pageant of Mexican national life corresponded perfectly with what I had in mind for art in the United States."[28] When Rivera arrived in San Francisco, Benton was already busy creating murals about United States history and culture, including scenes of the Westward Movement, Mississippi River boats, steel mills, and the Roaring Twenties.

By the time Rivera left the United States, mural making had caught fire, and buildings all over the country were being decorated with frescoes. From the Colt Tower in San Francisco to a new Justice Department building in Washington, D.C., artists everywhere were emulating Rivera's form. Perhaps in one sense, Rivera's visit north had been a disaster. But in a larger view, Diego Rivera had left an indelible impression on United States art.

THE PAINTER OF CONTROVERSY

In 1934, Rivera returned to his work on the frescoes in the National Palace. Now he painted the last section of the mural, entitling it "Mexico Today and Tomorrow." Near the center of this fresco, Rivera painted what he believed to be the causes of unhappiness for most Mexican citizens. Among these were the unfair use of power by political and religious leaders, and wealthy people's lack of concern for the poor. Around these pictures Rivera painted striking workers, poor farmers, and revolutionary soldiers. At the very top of the panel stands Karl

Marx, Rivera's solution to Mexico's strife. Marx is speaking to a group of ordinary citizens while pointing to a city in the distance. The city looks happy and peaceful, presumably so because it follows Marxist beliefs.

The stairway murals took Rivera nearly six years to complete, but the result was well worth the wait. Some critics believe the work shows Rivera at his best.[1] The project, however, taxed Rivera's stamina. It required an immense amount of imagination and artistic expertise as well as a bottomless well of strength and endurance. In a letter to a friend, Kahlo described Rivera's state when he finished the frescoes as "weak, thin, yellow, and morally exhausted."[2]

Furthermore, just as Rivera's art spoke of conflict, conflict dominated his personal life. His relationship with Kahlo was strained. While they were in Detroit, she had suffered a miscarriage, and she had been deeply disappointed.[3] Back in Mexico City, she was struck another blow when she learned that Rivera was having an affair with her sister.[4] Kahlo moved out of their new house, but returned a few months later. Although Rivera had hurt her terribly, she still adored him. During their separation she said she came to realize that she "loved him more than her own skin."[5] She now cared for him as he suffered through various illnesses, including glandular disorders and an infection in a tear duct. Even so, Rivera continued to see other women.[6] Consequently, Kahlo, too, had her own intimate relationships with others.[7]

Unfortunately, instability in his marriage was not the only problem in Rivera's personal life. His recent trip to the United States had again angered some of his friends. Rivera had been well paid for his work in the capitalist country, and many communists, including Siqueiros, felt he had betrayed his political ideals. At one meeting, the two artists argued. The evening ended with them waving guns at each other.

Now Rivera found himself without any mural commissions. But in the summer of 1936, an old friend, Alberto Pani, came to his rescue. Pani was building an elegant hotel in Mexico City, and he hired Rivera to decorate some of its walls. As had by now become his practice, Rivera used his art to express his political views. Because the murals would be in the hotel's dining and dancing hall, Rivera chose "the carnival of Mexican life" as his theme. A few of the frescoes he painted depicted Mexican folk festivals. Rivera also painted a contemporary carnival scene. But it was Rivera's last mural that received the most attention. In this panel, Rivera painted a masquerade ball attended by various government officials. The people at the party were wearing animal masks, but some could be identified by certain unique characteristics. The figure that caused the greatest anger was a general wearing a pig mask. This character was dubbed "General Pig" and was dancing with "Miss Mexico." As the two swirled around the ballroom floor, General Pig stole a piece of fruit from a basket that was fastened to Miss Mexico's back. Most people believed that the general was supposed to be Calles. The picture was Rivera's way of saying that the president had taken advantage of the Mexican people. Not surprisingly, Rivera's painting was highly offensive to Mexican authorities.

Suspecting the mural would cause trouble, Rivera had created his work on movable panels. This way if Pani did not want the frescoes, they would not have to be destroyed as the mural in the RCA building had. Indeed, Pani *was* unhappy. But instead of conferring with Rivera, he quietly hired other artists to paint over the insulting images. When Rivera heard that his murals had been changed, he was enraged. He took two pistols and stormed to the hotel. The police were called, and Rivera was thrown into jail for the night. But Rivera was not finished. He sued Pani in court, demanding that his frescoes be restored to their original condition. Rivera won his lawsuit, but Pani sold the panels.

Again, ill health plagued Rivera. In 1936, he was hospitalized several times for eye and kidney problems. These illnesses, of course, did not keep him from his art. While he recovered, he worked on sketches, oil paintings, watercolors, and portraits. Financially, the time was profitable, for there was always an abundance of people willing to buy a Rivera canvas.

Rivera's illnesses did not keep him from his politics, either. Because he still had not been allowed to rejoin Mexico's Communist party, Rivera joined a group that followed one of Russia's revolutionary leaders, Leon Trotsky. Trotsky had been second-in-command to Lenin during the Russian Revolution of 1917. When Lenin died in 1924, Trotsky found himself engaged in a power struggle with a man named Joseph Stalin. Stalin won, and took control of the Russian government. Fearing Trotsky would try to overthrow him, Stalin banished Trotsky from the country. Since then, Trotsky had lived in Turkey, France, and Norway. Now the Norwegian government told Trotsky he must leave the country. With nowhere to go, he turned to the Trotsky organization in Mexico for help. Rivera agreed to aid the former Russian leader, and in 1937, Trotsky and his wife arrived in Mexico. Rivera and Kahlo were there to greet them. They escorted the couple to Kahlo's childhood home in Coyoacán where the Trotskys would live for the next two years.

In the meantime, Kahlo had continued to paint. Her reputation as a talented artist had grown, and in 1938 she had her first solo art exhibition in New York City. She traveled to the United States alone, where her work was well received.[8] Next she went to Paris.

There she met other artists, including Rivera's old acquaintance, Picasso. Even though the two men had parted on unfriendly terms, Picasso greeted Kahlo warmly. When Kahlo returned to Mexico, Rivera announced that he wanted to divorce her. Again, Kahlo was devastated. Referring to her marriage, Kahlo once confided to a friend, "I have suffered two serious accidents in my life, one in which a streetcar ran over me . . . The other accident is Diego."[9]

Rivera continued to paint. However, the recent mural incident involving Pani's hotel hung heavy in the air, making Mexican officials afraid to hire Rivera to create more murals.[10] So in 1940, Rivera participated in a unique exhibition in San Francisco. There he painted at an international fair while thousands of people watched. Appropriately, the exhibition was called "Art in Action." As had happened during his first visit to the United States, Rivera was welcomed and entertained by San Francisco's wealthy and famous.

But in spite of all of the attention, Rivera was lonely. In his own curious way, he still loved Kahlo.[11] Perhaps this was because she understood him so well. Kahlo had once said, "I cannot speak of Diego as my husband . . . He never has been, nor will he ever be, anybody's husband . . . To Diego painting is everything. He prefers his work to anything else in the world."[12] Near the end of his stay in San Francisco, Rivera invited Kahlo to join him, and she came

Frida Kahlo described her husband as an "immense baby with an amiable but sad-looking face."

immediately. The two remarried on Rivera's fifty-fourth birthday.

Soon after Rivera and Kahlo arrived home in 1941, Kahlo moved out of their San Angel house and into her old home in Coyoacán. There, she felt, she could live a life more independent of Rivera.[13] She redecorated the house, surrounding herself with indigenous art, folk art, and dolls. One of her favorite types of decorations were huge papier-mâché Judas figures, which Mexican folk artists fashioned for traditional Easter celebrations. Rivera, too, liked Judas figures, and he often added his own to the collection at Coyoacán. Rivera also enjoyed being with Kahlo, and so divided his time between Coyoacán and his art studio.

Rivera did not lack for work. So many requests for his easel paintings flowed in that even a man with Rivera's stamina could not possibly accept them all. He was able to paint many, though, and was well paid for them. As usual, much of the money he earned was donated to a communist organization or used to buy pre-Conquest art. Yet, for all his busyness, Rivera longed for walls. Financially, he was better off creating paintings. He only earned about ten dollars a day painting murals, and from these wages he had to buy materials and pay his assistants. But frescoes were Rivera's favorite medium and without them, he felt empty.[14]

By 1943, the memory of Rivera's recent hotel incident had finally faded, and once more he was offered public walls in Mexico. Now Rivera was hired to paint additional frescoes at the National Palace. There, on hallways throughout the building, Rivera created murals portraying some of Mexico's earliest civilizations. One mural was called "The Great City of Tenochtitlán," and depicted the Aztec capital that had once flourished on the very ground below the National Palace.

Tenochtitlán had been built in the mid-1300s on an island. When the Spaniards conquered the Aztecs, they filled in the surrounding lake and built Mexico City on the site. Rivera's mural depicts Tenochtitlán just before the Spaniards arrived. In the foreground, native men and women trade corn, fruit, poultry, and flowers at a busy market. Behind the market, the city stretches into the distance, divided into blocks by man-made canals. Some of these blocks are family farms where rich harvests of corn, beans, squash, and tomatoes grow. To one side of the mural, a raised-earth road connects the island city to the mainland. At the horizon, mountains rise in soft pinks and purples. Between them and the market occasional pyramids rise above the city, with long rows of stairs leading to temples at their tops. This was where the Aztecs prayed. It was also where they practiced human sacrifice, and the steps of two pyramids are stained with blood. Even so, Rivera's fresco is graceful and poetic, and somehow softer than his usual political murals. Of it, Rivera once said, "One could not love a subject so deeply without painting it well."[15]

During the same time, Rivera was working on another dream. He was planning a museum to house his constantly growing collection of pre-Conquest Mexican art. The museum he designed for the indigenous works would be called Anahuacalli, meaning the house of Anahuac. Anahuac is one name for the geographic area that the Aztecs inhabited before the arrival of the Spaniards. Rivera chose a site near Coyoacán for his museum. Wanting the building to look as if it had grown out of the earth, he designed a three-story structure that resembled an ancient Mexican pyramid. To help it blend into its surroundings, Rivera's museum would be constructed of stone from the region. Rivera's pre-Conquest sculptures would be displayed on the museum's main floor. The second and third levels would be Rivera's home and studio. But Anahuacalli proceeded slowly. Its construction funds came directly out of Rivera's pockets, and he could only hire workers when he had extra money.

In 1947, Rivera was asked to paint at another hotel being built in Mexico City. The Hotel del Prado sat near one of Mexico's oldest parks, the Alameda. Established in 1592, Alameda Park had been enjoyed by generations of Mexicans. Rivera, himself, remembered listening to band concerts there as a child. But the Alameda had also been the scene of turmoil. In its earliest days, officials had burned victims of the Inquisition in a crematorium at one end of the park. Numerous political demonstrations had been held there in the centuries that followed. Even Zapata's rebel troops had camped in the park during the Revolution. In his mural, Rivera combined significant people from the park's history with significant people from his personal life. The entire group stood together in Alameda Park as if they were posing for a photograph. Obviously, this group could only have been together in a dream, so Rivera named his work "Dream of a Sunday Afternoon in the Alameda."

At first glance, the mural looks lighthearted. But its quaint, festive mood hides some deeper meanings. Rivera painted himself as a child in the center of the fresco. A frog and a snake peer from young Rivera's jacket pockets, and he holds the hand of a calavera that is standing next to him. The calavera rests its other hand on the arm of José Guadalupe Posada, the artist who had the strongest influence on Rivera when he was a student. An adult Kahlo poses behind Rivera, looking as if she might be his mother. Nearby is the aunt who had once taken Rivera to church in Guanajuato. By her side stands the wife of Mexico's former president, Porfirio Díaz. It was Mrs. Díaz who had opened Rivera's art exhibit at the San Carlos Academy in 1910. José Vasconcelos also appears in the mural, as does Rivera's ex-wife Guadalupe Marín, and the couple's two daughters. In the background, Zapata strikes a gallant pose on a rearing horse, and Díaz gazes solemnly at the crowd. In another section of the picture, a poor family gets thrown out of the park by a policeman.

Had Rivera left the mural as it was, it might have been received as a playful, yet thought-provoking painting. But characteristically, Rivera did not. Instead, he added Ignacio Ramirez to the mural, an atheist who had encouraged Mexico's government to separate itself from the Catholic Church in the mid-1800s. Back then, Benito Júarez was Mexico's president, and he, too, was against letting the church govern the country. Rivera painted Júarez standing near Ramirez. Then, as if to ensure a scandal, Rivera painted a scroll in Ramirez's hand that read, "God does not exist."

Mexico City nearly exploded. The Catholic archbishop refused to bless the hotel, something of a disaster in a country where a majority of the people were devout Catholics. Catholic students raided the hotel and scratched out the words on Rivera's mural. To further emphasize their point, they gashed at the portrait of Rivera. Many citizens who did not actively protest Rivera's fresco were also offended. One said, "We know Rivera is our greatest painter, but he hurts our feelings."[16]

In this section of "Dream of a Sunday Afternoon in the Alameda," Rivera painted the following people (left to right): an unknown newsboy, a famous Mexican writer (in top hat), Rivera's aunt, Mrs. Díaz, Rivera as a child, Frida Kahlo, a calavera, and José Guadalupe Posada.

Ironically, Rivera was serving on a government committee at the time called the Commission of Mural Painting. One of the committee's functions was to protect painters and their art from censorship and vandalism. José Clemente Orozco and David Alfaro Siqueiros were the other two committee members. Predictably, neither would allow Rivera's mural to be destroyed. So the owner of the Hotel del Prado blocked the fresco with a red screen. The mural would remain unseen and forgotten for almost a decade. Of course, the same could not be said of Rivera.

CHAPTER EIGHT

RIVERA'S GIFTS TO THE WORLD

At times it seemed as if Rivera sat in the eye of each hurricane he created. Although wild winds of controversy raged all around him, he emerged from most storms unscathed. The Hotel del Prado hurricane passed, too, leaving Rivera's artistic reputation unharmed. For despite the controversy he so often provoked, despite the enemies he made, Mexico could not deny the great accomplishments of Diego Rivera, the artist. In 1949, Mexico's National Art Museum planned an extravagant exhibition of his work entitled "Fifty Years of the Art of Diego Rivera."

This huge show displayed more than one thousand pieces of Rivera's art from every period of his career. Before it was over, thousands of people had filed through the exhibit halls to see what one writer described as "The magnificent accomplishments of [Mexico's] great artist."[1]

Now more than sixty years old, Rivera stayed as busy as ever. He continued to turn out dozens of portraits commissioned by wealthy people and he sold hundreds of drawings and easel paintings to others. Rivera now painted with confidence and speed, practically mass-producing the paintings he sold. His most popular works were pictures of flowers or of the Mexican landscape. Friends and tourists constantly streamed through his studio, and he spoke with them politely and patiently. Yet he rarely stopped working.

As before, Rivera gave his money away almost as fast as he earned it. Sometimes he stuffed a handful of dollars into a beggar's hand without bothering to see how much he was giving away.[2] Whatever was left went toward buying his pre-Conquest art treasures, and now, toward building Anahuacalli. Completing the half-finished museum had become more important to him than any of his paintings.[3] Rivera spent many hours considering where and how each pre-Conquest piece should be displayed. Most of the sculptures were grouped according to style, meaning, and age.

Rivera also spent a lot of time decorating Anahuacalli.

A skilled portrait artist, Rivera painted this rendition of himself in 1949. He named it "The Ravages of Time."

Large sections of the building were adorned with mosaic designs. In one of these designs, a serpent speaks the word "toad" (Kahlo's affectionate nickname for Rivera) in Mayan hieroglyphics. Next to his nickname is the Aztec sign for the date of Rivera's birth. Rivera also created a mosaic mural on the ceiling of the building's first floor. Here, Tlaloc, the Aztec god of rain, hovers in a cloud-like pattern of white stones.

A mosaic Tlaloc appeared in another work Rivera was making at the time. This art had been commissioned by the Mexico City water treatment facility. In it, Rivera hoped to express life's dependence on water and show gratitude to the people who worked at the water treatment facility. The project was really two different pieces of artwork. One was a sculpture of Tlaloc made out of earth. Rivera decorated the top of it with different-colored rocks. For the second part of the project, Rivera planned to paint a mural inside a large water basin. The major obstacle in this work was developing a paint that would not dissolve in the water. Rivera devised a paint that he thought would last and went to work. On the tank's bottom he painted one-celled organisms. Along the lower walls, Rivera painted more complex life forms, which looked as if they were evolving inside the tank. As Rivera painted higher and higher onto the walls, life evolved further and further. Finally, near the top of the tank were a man and a woman. Regrettably, Rivera was wrong about the hardiness of his paint, and the mural began to erode within the decade.

In 1953, Rivera worked in mosaics again. This time he decorated a huge wall outside of a Mexico City movie theater. On it, Rivera created a brightly colored mural of popular people from Mexican history. Between work on his mosaics, paintings, and Anahuacalli, Rivera painted at the National Palace, too. He had now completed eleven hallway panels there, each one depicting life in ancient Mexico.

Unfortunately, Kahlo's health had been poor during the past decade. She had suffered from several illnesses including anemia, depression, and ever-present back and leg pains.[4] She had been operated on, put into corsets (a type of body cast), and given a bone graft. Nothing seemed to help, and she sometimes turned to drugs or alcohol to ease her suffering.[5] When she was honored with a one-person exhibit at the National Institute of Fine Arts in 1953, she was very ill. She went anyway, arriving in an ambulance and spending the entire exhibit on a bed. Her show was so popular, it had to be extended a full month to accommodate everyone who wanted to see her work.

But Kahlo's professional victory was overshadowed by her poor health. In August, she had to have one leg amputated due to gangrene. After the operation, she again became depressed.[6] Rivera hired nurses to take care of her and continued to work. Occasionally, one would interrupt him to report that Kahlo was especially depressed. Then Rivera would go to his wife and comfort her.

In July 1954, Kahlo attended a demonstration protesting United States involvement in Guatemala. Rivera pushed her in a wheelchair amidst thousands of other marchers. After the outing, Kahlo caught pneumonia. Once again, she was bedridden and her condition grew worse. Frida Kahlo died on July 13 with Rivera at her side. A friend standing near Rivera at the time noted that he "became an old man in a few hours."[7] Rivera would later call the day of Kahlo's death the most tragic day of his life.[8]

In September of the same year, Rivera was finally readmitted into Mexico's Communist party. For the next several months, he painted at an easel, frequently working on commissioned portraits. One of Rivera's most well-known portraits, "Portrait of Dolores Olmeda," was painted during this period. Olmeda was a friend of Rivera's and owned many of his paintings.

Rivera married again in 1955. His new wife, Emma Hurtado, had been his art dealer since 1946. Together they traveled to the Soviet Union on an invitation from the Moscow Fine Arts Academy. While in Moscow, Rivera received treatments for cancer at a hospital. When he returned to Mexico in April 1956, he looked weak, but he told newspaper reporters that he was thinking about several new projects. "I should live ten years more," he said. "Right now my fingers are itching to start my next mural."[9] Curiously, one of the first things Rivera did after arriving home was to paint out the "God does not exist" declaration on his mural at the Hotel del Prado. Then he proclaimed that he was a Catholic. Apparently, the man who had once called worshippers stupid and who had frequently painted criticisms of the Catholic Church into his murals had come back from Russia with a new view of religion.

The Mexican government declared Rivera's seventieth birthday a special holiday, and he was honored with a celebration. Afterward, Rivera continued to paint, sketch, and plan major projects, even though he was in poor health. Then, in September 1957, a blood clot and swelling in his veins paralyzed his right arm. Rivera refused to go to a hospital. Instead, he stayed at home in bed with two unfinished paintings beside him. One was of a smiling Russian child; the other of his granddaughter. Rivera wanted his work near him so he could paint as soon as he could pick up a brush.[10] He never had the chance.

On November 24, Diego Rivera died in his sleep from heart failure. His body was taken to the Palace of Fine Arts where it lay in state while twenty thousand people came to pay Rivera their respects. Among them were notables from all over the world, including the famous Mexican artists, Dr. Atl and David Alfaro Siqueiros. Rivera was buried at a prestigious Mexican cemetery, the Cemetery of Dolores, in a special area there that was reserved for national heroes. Appropriately, he was laid to rest next to another one of Mexico's "Big Three" artists, José Clemente Orozco.

In spite of leaving several projects incomplete when he died, Rivera's legacy was rich. He left Anahuacalli and its sixty thousand pieces of pre-Conquest art to the people of his nation. Experts still consider Anahuacalli's collection to be one of the finest of its kind. Many of these pieces might have been lost forever had it not been for Rivera's determination to preserve them for future generations. A stone at Anahuacalli's entrance is inscribed with Rivera's words and purpose: "I return to the people the artistic heritage I was able to redeem from their ancestors."[11]

In addition, Rivera left a massive amount of artwork to his homeland. Back in 1949, one writer had added together the total area Rivera's murals covered. She found that if each fresco were only three feet wide, the work would stretch from the top of the Empire State Building to the bottom—ten and a half times![12] And this number did not even include Rivera's easel paintings, mosaics, or the work he did after 1949.

Rivera's murals can still be seen on buildings around Mexico City. Most are available to the general public, including his grand works at the National Palace and the Ministry of Education. In addition, Mexico's

National Art Museum owns the mural Rivera painted at his friend's hotel and his repainted version of the RCA building fresco. The Palace of Cortés still stands in Cuernavaca. It is now a museum, and Rivera's murals there remain as vivid reminders of Mexico's past. In marked contrast to the days when Rivera's murals were being mocked or destroyed by a disapproving public, they are now treated with the utmost care. For instance, when Rivera's fresco at the Hotel del Prado was cracking because of the hotel's shifting foundation and earthquake tremors, experts were consulted to save it. The wall, weighing nearly nine tons, was placed section by section onto a specially made steel boxcar. Rails were laid and the fresco was carefully transported from the hotel's dance hall to its lobby. Now the fresco is displayed there, safe from further damage.

In addition to his murals, Rivera also left behind a wealth of easel paintings and sketches. While many of these are scattered among museums and private collections throughout the world, the Museum of Plastic Arts in Mexico City boasts an exceptional collection. So does the Diego Rivera Museum in Guanajuato, Mexico, which is housed in Rivera's childhood home. The first floor of the residence has been restored to look as it might have when Rivera lived there. The second and third floors are devoted to displaying ninety pieces of Rivera's work.

The mural revival inspired by Diego Rivera and other Mexican artists lives on today. United States artist Leo Tanguma created the mural shown on these two pages at the Denver International Airport in Denver, Colorado. It is called "Dream of Peace: In Peace and Harmony with Nature."

The dancing woman on the right is a portrait of Tanguma's mother as a young woman.

Museums in the United States from San Francisco to New York City also own some of Rivera's work. And, as in Mexico, his United States murals are being carefully preserved. "Allegory of California" is in the same San Francisco building where it was painted. The building, however, is now called the City Club of San Francisco. The fresco in which Rivera painted himself creating a mural is at the San Francisco Art Institute. Rivera's "Art in Action" mural, entitled "Pan-American Unity," is on display at the City College of San Francisco. The Detroit Institute of Arts murals remain exactly as they were painted and thousands of people view them each year.

In addition to artwork, Rivera also left the world several important ideas. First was his deep belief that art should be for everyone in a society. Another was his notion that art should dignify the common person. Finally, Rivera believed that art must be meaningful to the people who view it.

Years after Rivera's death, his influence can still be seen in art in the United States. In the 1960s, artists painted murals about the struggle for civil rights and their feelings about the Vietnam War. Other artists painted murals celebrating ethnic pride. Today murals are found everywhere in the United States, and many express a particular opinion about a topic. Of course, people do not always like the message behind a piece of art. Rivera himself had frequently angered people with the personal opinions he expressed in his art. But few would argue that Rivera's work was hollow. Neither was it temporary. United States interest in Rivera's work continues today, and museums still hold exhibitions of his work. Private collectors, too, maintain enthusiasm for his art. In fact, almost thirty years after his death, one of his easel paintings sold for nearly half a million dollars![13]

Rivera's driving ambition was to combine superior art with important social principles. The road to this accomplishment was not always smooth. But neither was it boring. According to Rivera's accounts, his days were filled with spectacular adventures. Some people believe that Rivera exaggerated the stories he told about his life. Many even accused him of having difficulty separating fact from fiction.[14] But the people who knew Rivera best thought that his autobiographical tales all contained a piece of truth about the road he had traveled. One friend described Rivera's life as fabulous: fabulously good, fabulously bad, fabulously interesting.[15] Whatever Rivera did, he did with exuberance. Whatever Rivera felt, he felt with gusto. And perhaps it was this ability to feel so deeply that made Rivera the monumental artist he was.

Chronology

1886—Diego María Rivera is born in Guanajuato, Mexico.

1896—Rivera begins art classes at Mexico City's San Carlos Academy of Fine Arts.

1907—Having received a government scholarship, Rivera travels to Spain to study art. During the next several years, he wanders throughout Europe to paint.

1913— Rivera adopts cubism, a unique style of abstract painting.

1918 Rivera denounces cubism in his search for a
–1920 more meaningful artistic style. He travels to Italy to study the works of Renaissance masters and is particularly impressed with the murals of Michelangelo.

1921— Rivera returns to Mexico and begins his mural-making career under the sponsorship of Mexico's minister of Education, José Vasconcelos.

1922— Rivera becomes the common-law husband of Guadalupe Marín. He also joins the Communist party of Mexico.

1923— Rivera is constantly busy, painting murals at
-1928 the Ministry of Education building and at an
agricultural college in Chapingo, Mexico. Most
of these paintings depict the lives of everyday
Mexicans. Marín and Rivera separate.

1929— Rivera marries Frida Kahlo, then begins
painting murals in Mexico City's National
Palace. Rivera is expelled from the Communist
party because of philosophical disagreements.
He travels to Cuernavaca, Mexico, at the end
of the year to paint at the Palace of Cortés.

1930— Making his first visit to the United States,
-1933 Rivera paints in San Francisco, California, and
Detroit, Michigan. He then begins a mural in
New York City that causes so much controversy
that it is never completed.

1934— Returning to Mexico, Rivera finishes his murals
above the stairway at the National Palace.

1936— Another controversy arises over murals Rivera
paints in an exclusive Mexico City hotel.

1936— In disfavor and ill health, Rivera concentrates
-1942 on easel landscapes and portraits. He also
begins planning Anahuacalli, a museum that
will house his large collection of pre-Conquest
Mexican art.

1943— Rivera paints at the National Palace again and
-1947 completes another controversial mural at a
local hotel.

1949—Mexico honors Rivera with an extensive showing of his work entitled, "Fifty Years of the Art of Diego Rivera." Afterward, Rivera continues to paint, but also experiments with designs in mosaic.

1954—Frida Kahlo dies. Rivera is readmitted into the Communist party.

1955— Rivera marries Emma Hurtado.

1957— On November 24, Diego Rivera dies of heart failure.

CHAPTER NOTES

CHAPTER 1

    1. Alma M. Reed, *The Mexican Muralists* (New York: Crown Publishers, 1960), p. 83.

    2. Laurence E. Schmeckebier, *Modern Mexican Art* (Westport, Conn.: Greenwood Press, 1971), p. 139.

    3. Cynthia Newman Helms, ed., *Diego Rivera: A Retrospective* (New York: W.W. Norton, 1986), p. 261.

    4. Diego Rivera with Gladys March, *Diego Rivera: My Art, My Life* (New York: The Citadel Press, 1960), p. 288.

    5. Oriana Baddeley, "Rivera Revived," *Art History*, June 1988, p. 271.

CHAPTER 2

    1. Ramón Favela, *Diego Rivera: The Cubist Years* (Phoenix: Phoenix Art Museum, 1984), p. 7.

    2. Florence Arquin, *Diego Rivera, The Shaping of an Artist* (Norman, Okla.: University of Oklahoma Press, 1971), p. 7.

    3. Cynthia Newman Helms, ed., *Diego Rivera: A Retrospective* (New York: W.W. Norton, 1986), p. 25.

    4. Diego Rivera with Gladys March, *Diego Rivera: My Art, My Life* (New York: The Citadel Press, 1960), p. 24.

    5. Ibid., pp. 26–27.

6. Ibid., p. 34.

7. Hayden Herrera, *Frida: A Biography of Frida Kahlo* (New York: Harper and Row, 1983), p. 81.

8. Jean Charlot, *Mexican Art and the Academy of San Carlos, 1785–1915* (Austin, Tex.: University of Texas Press, 1962), p. 140.

9. Arquin, p. 10.

10. Favela, p. 20.

11. "The Long Voyage Home," *Time*, April 4, 1949, p. 56.

12. Ibid.

13. Favela, p. 20.

14. Charlot, p. 140.

15. Alma M. Reed, *The Mexican Muralists* (New York: Crown Publishers, 1960), p. 14.

16. Arquin, p. 37.

17. Charlot, p. 142.

18. Bertram D. Wolfe, *The Fabulous Life of Diego Rivera* (New York: Stein and Day, 1963), p. 38.

19. Ibid.

20. Charlot, p. 152.

CHAPTER 3

1. Bertram D. Wolfe, *The Fabulous Life of Diego Rivera* (New York: Stein and Day, 1963), p. 47.

2. Ibid.

3. Diego Rivera with Gladys March, *Diego Rivera: My Art, My Life* (New York: The Citadel Press, 1960), p. 55.

4. James Cockcroft, *Diego Rivera* (New York: Chelsea House Publishers, 1991), p. 36.

5. Ibid., p. 37.

6. Rivera with March, p. 65.

7. Ibid., p. 66.

8. Ibid., p. 76.

9. Cockcroft, p. 38.

10. Ramón Favela, *Diego Rivera: The Cubist Years* (Phoenix: Phoenix Art Museum, 1984), p. 24.

11. Laurence E. Schmeckebier, *Modern Mexican Art* (Westport, Conn.: Greenwood Press, 1971), pp. 132–133.

12. Wolfe, p. 417.

13. Schmeckebier, p. 112.

14. Favela, p. 29.

15. Cynthia Newman Helms, ed., *Diego Rivera: A Retrospective* (New York: W.W. Norton, 1986), p. 34.

CHAPTER 4

1. Bertram D. Wolfe, *The Fabulous Life of Diego Rivera* (New York: Stein and Day, 1963), p. 94.

2. Ramón Favela, *Diego Rivera: The Cubist Years* (Phoenix: Phoenix Art Museum, 1984), p. 62.

3. Ibid., p. 76.

4. Ibid., p. 93.

5. Ibid., p. 110.

6. Ibid.

7. Ibid.

8. "The Long Voyage Home," *Time*, April 4, 1949, p. 56.

9. Diego Rivera with Gladys March, *Diego Rivera: My Art, My Life* (New York: The Citadel Press, 1960), p. 294.

10. James Cockcroft, *Diego Rivera* (New York: Chelsea House Publishers, 1991), p. 58.

11. Cynthia Newman Helms, ed., *Diego Rivera: A Retrospective* (New York: W.W. Norton, 1986), p. 45.

12. Florence Arquin, *Diego Rivera, The Shaping of an Artist* (Norman, Okla.: University of Oklahoma Press, 1971), p. 86.

13. MacKinley Helm, *Modern Mexican Painters* (Freeport, N.Y.: Books for Libraries Press, 1968), p. 41.

14. Ibid.

15. Ibid.

16. Arquin, p. 86.

17. "The Long Voyage Home," p. 56.

18. The Museum of Modern Art, *Twenty Centuries of Mexican Art* (New York: Museum of Modern Art, 1972), p. 138.

19. Arquin, pp. 139–143.

20. Ibid., p. 143.

21. Rivera with March, p. 124.

22. Helms, p. 19.

CHAPTER 5

1. The Museum of Modern Art, *Twenty Centuries of Mexican Art* (New York: Museum of Modern Art, 1972), p. 139.

2. Barbara Mujica, "A Turning Point in Modernism," *Américas*, vol. 44, no. 2, 1992, p. 30.

3. Ibid.

4. Martha Zamora, *Frida Kahlo: The Brush of Anguish* (San Francisco: Chronicle Books, 1990), p. 37.

5. Diego Rivera with Gladys March, *Diego Rivera: My Art, My Life* (New York: The Citadel Press, 1960), p. 297.

6. Laurance P. Hurlburt, *The Mexican Muralists in the United States* (Albuquerque: University of New Mexico Press, 1989), p. 3.

7. The Museum of Modern Art, p. 139.

8. MacKinley Helm, *Modern Mexican Painters* (Freeport, N.Y.: Books for Libraries Press, 1968), p. 46.

9. Bertram D. Wolfe, *The Fabulous Life of Diego Rivera* (New York: Stein and Day, 1963), p. 182.

10. Rivera with March, pp. 137, 138.

11. Laurence E. Schmeckebier, *Modern Mexican Art* (Westport, Conn.: Greenwood Press, 1971), p. 38.

12. Rivera with March, p. 299.

13. Alma M. Reed, *The Mexican Muralists* (New York: Crown Publishers, 1960), p. 78.

14. Hayden Herrera, *Frida: A Biography of Frida Kahlo* (New York: Harper and Row, 1983), p. 85.

15. James Cockcroft, *Diego Rivera* (New York: Chelsea House Publishers, 1991), p. 73.

16. Wolfe, p. 169.

17. Ibid., p. 179.

18. Zamora, p. 34.

19. Ibid.

20. Herrera, p. 102.

21. Ibid., p. 115.

22. Ibid.

CHAPTER 6

1. Bertram D. Wolfe, *The Fabulous Life of Diego Rivera* (New York: Stein and Day, 1963), pp. 280–281.

2. Ibid.

3. Hayden Herrera, *Frida: A Biography of Frida Kahlo* (New York: Harper and Row, 1983), p. 115.

4. "Rivera Says His Art is Red Propaganda," *The New York Times*, May 14, 1933, Section 1, p. 1.

5. Laurance P. Hurlburt, *The Mexican Muralists in the United States* (Albuquerque: University of New Mexico Press, 1989), p. 100.

6. Laurence E. Schmeckebier, *Modern Mexican Art* (Westport, Conn.: Greenwood Press, 1971), p. 145.

7. Cynthia Newman Helms, ed., *Diego Rivera: A Retrospective* (New York: W.W. Norton, 1986), p. 79.

8. Schmeckebier, p. 146.

9. Hurlburt, pp. 138, 140.

10. Helms, p. 215.

11. Ibid., p. 210.

12. Florence Arquin, *Diego Rivera, The Shaping of an Artist* (Norman, Okla.: University of Oklahoma Press, 1971), p. 9.

13. Helms, p. 210.

14. Hurlburt, p. 254.

15. Ibid., p. 166.

16. "Rivera's Wrong Pew," editorial, *The New York Times*, May 16, 1933, p. 16.

17. Hurlburt, p. 169.

18. Schmeckebier, p. 149.

19. Hurlburt, p. 169.

20. Ibid.

21. "Art Row Pressed by Rivera Friends," *The New York Times*, May 18, 1933, p. 22.

22. Diego Rivera with Gladys March, *Diego Rivera: My Art, My Life* (New York: The Citadel Press, 1960), p. 210.

23. Schmeckebier, p. 150.

24. Ibid.

25. Letter to the Editor by Harry D. Robbins, "The Rivera Murals," *The New York Times*, May 14, 1933, Section 4, p. 5.

26. "Art Row Pressed By Rivera Friends," p. 22.

27. Hurlburt, p. 174.

28. Helms, p. 160.

CHAPTER 7

1. Cynthia Newman Helms, ed., *Diego Rivera: A Retrospective* (New York: W.W. Norton, 1986), p. 263.

2. Hayden Herrera, *Frida: A Biography of Frida Kahlo* (New York: Harper and Row, 1983), p. 181.

3. Sarah M. Lowe, *Frida Kahlo* (New York: Universe Publishing, 1991), p. 65.

4. Herrera, p. 181.

5. Martha Zamora, *Frida Kahlo: The Brush of Anguish* (San Francisco: Chronicle Books, 1990), p. 50.

6. Herrera, p. 186.

7. Zamora, p. 50.

8. Erika Billeter, ed., *The World of Frida Kahlo* (Houston, Tex.: Museum of Fine Arts, 1993), p. 254.

9. Zamora, p. 37.

10. Bertram D. Wolfe, *The Fabulous Life of Diego Rivera* (New York: Stein and Day, 1963), p. 362.

11. Herrera, p. 298.

12. Diego Rivera with Gladys March, *Diego Rivera: My Art, My Life* (New York: The Citadel Press, 1960), pp. 301, 303.

13. Zamora, p. 70.

14. Wolfe, p. 362.

15. Rivera with March, pp. 249–250.

16. "The Long Voyage Home," *Time*, April 4, 1949, p. 62.

CHAPTER 8

1. *Diego Rivera Museum, Anahuacalli* (The Organizing Committee of the Games of the XIX Olympiad: Mexico, 1970), p. 12.

2. "The Long Voyage Home," *Time*, April 4, 1949, pp. 63–64.

3. Ibid., p. 64.

4. Erika Billeter, ed., *The World of Frida Kahlo* (Houston, Tex.: Museum of Fine Arts, 1993), pp. 256–261.

5. Martha Zamora, *Frida Kahlo: The Brush of Anguish* (San Francisco: Chronicle Books, 1990), p. 118.

6. Ibid., pp. 126, 130.

7. Hayden Herrera, *Frida: A Biography of Frida Kahlo* (New York: Harper and Row, 1983), p. 433.

8. Ibid., p. 438.

9. Bertram D. Wolfe, *The Fabulous Life of Diego Rivera* (New York: Stein and Day, 1963), p. 408.

10. Ibid., p. 412.

11. *Diego Rivera Museum*, Anahuacalli, p. 18.

12. Wolfe, p. 429.

13. Laurance P. Hurlburt, *The Mexican Muralists in the United States* (Albuquerque: University of New Mexico Press, 1989), p. 291.

14. Cynthia Newman Helms, ed., *Diego Rivera: A Retrospective* (New York: W.W. Norton, 1986), p. 19.

15. Wolfe, p. 6.

FURTHER READING

Cockcroft, James D. *Diego Rivera*. New York: Chelsea House Publishers, 1991.

Cruz, Bárbara C. *Frida Kahlo: Portrait of a Mexican Painter*. Springfield, N.J.: Enslow Publishers, 1996.

Favela, Ramón. *Diego Rivera, The Cubist Years*. Phoenix: Phoenix Art Museum, 1984.

Helms, Cynthia Newman, ed. *Diego Rivera: A Retrospective*. New York: W.W. Norton, 1986.

Rivera, Diego, with Gladys March. *Diego Rivera: My Art, My Life*. New York: The Citadel Press, 1960.

Wolfe, Bertram D. *The Fabulous Life of Diego Rivera*. New York: Stein and Day, 1963.

Zamora, Martha. *The Brush of Anguish*. San Francisco: Chronicle Books, 1990.

INDEX